DURING the Dissertation

A Textual Mentor for Doctoral Students in the Process of Writing

Christine Pearson Casanave

University of Michigan Press
Ann Arbor

Dedicated to doctoral students around the world who are persisting.

Published in the United States of America
The University of Michigan Press
Manufactured in the United States of America

♾ Printed on acid-free paper

ISBN-13: 978-0-472-03790-2
ISBN-13: 978-0-472-12841-9 (ebook)

2023 2022 2021 2020 4 3 2 1

Contents

Acknowledgments

As always, academic books don't get written without help from others, even when they are single-authored. Although it sometimes feels like I have worked in solitude, I realize that the work could not have been done if encouragement, advice, and commentary had not been generously provided by others. Stephanie Vandrick is at the top of the list of the usual gang of supporters—her encouragement and never-give-up attitude kept me going when I felt stalled, and her confidence in me as a scholar and writer picked up my spirits as it has in the past. Merrill Swain graciously read some chapters and provided insightful commentary, even though she swears she is no longer doing academic work. Her insights are invaluable. Also, several students in her SCOLAR study group read a draft of most of the chapters and provided helpful comments from their valuable firsthand perspectives as doctoral students—thanks to Art Babayants, Yuliya Desyatova, Justine Jun, Jennifer Burton, Michael Kozlowski, Matt Bury, and Bruce Russell.

Several of my current and past doctoral students who are featured in some chapters also read some chapter drafts and helped me present their experiences in ways that rang true to them. I am grateful to them as well as to the colleagues who contributed ideas and anecdotes (Mayumi Asaba, Dwight Atkinson, Kathi Bailey, Deborah Crusan, Natasha Hashimoto, John Hedgcock, Matt Prior, Lisa Russell-Pinson, Scott Shinall, among others). Were it not for the students and colleagues who shared experiences with me, this book would never have been written.

I am grateful, too, to Robert Kohls for his comments and for our ongoing discussions about "good writing," and what this elusive concept might mean in academia, and to Yongyan Li, whose reciprocal mentoring from afar has kept both of us going over the years. Marina Romani, friend of 48 years and now at rest in the cemetery near my neighborhood, always supported my efforts to use language in beautiful ways, as I did hers, but I am not the poet that she was.

Fresh air was provided by the library staff at the Middlebury Institute of International Studies in Monterey, California, who patiently opened windows for me on the sometimes stuffy second floor where I sat nearly every afternoon month after month drafting and proofing, and sometimes just pretending to draft and proof when the juices weren't flowing. Everyone always greeted me with a smile and sent me home with one too.

Finally, thanks to the reviewers enlisted by Kelly Sippell at the University of Michigan Press, who provided feedback on the manuscript and, more specifically, to Kelly herself for her faith in me, her patience, and her professionalism.

Introduction

Breathe deeply. Look inward. Look outward. Find your center and your purpose. Do this regularly in the coming months as you write (and re-write) your dissertation.

And consult this small book, which follows from a previous "textual mentor," *Before the Dissertation* (University of Michigan Press, 2014). Like the earlier book, it is written primarily to be a companion for doctoral dissertation writers who are doing qualitative or mixed methods work in fields related to language education. These are the methods and areas of inquiry I know best. From my experience and reading, I find that qualitative projects can be messier and less template-like than quantitative studies, and so potentially the source of more anxiety for dissertation writers, hence the usefulness of a book like this one. Nevertheless, the issues facing all doctoral writers are similar, including those who are writing dissertations with a quantitative approach or dissertations by publication. This book could also be used by writers of masters' theses in these fields and other social sciences, as many of the same issues pertain to both masters and doctoral level writers. (Note that in Europe and elsewhere, the terms *doctoral thesis* and *master's dissertation* are used. In this book, I follow the North American convention of referring to the single-document doctoral project as a dissertation.) For all writers, this book is meant to be consulted once actual writing has begun, in other words, when students are no longer struggling to find a topic, designing their project, or collecting data. Instead, they are analyzing, drafting, revising, polishing, and probably fretting, deleting, reconstructing, and all the while losing sleep.

For the most part, the book addresses challenges that graduate students face who are writing a single major document based on one main project rather than those who are compiling several previously published articles, as is accepted in some doctoral programs. Most of my anecdotes are from such students and sources, and because of my particular background and interests, I draw mainly on qualitative projects of the sort my students have done or that I have read about. However, I must note here that the single-authored monograph style of dissertation, which first appeared in medieval Europe, is likely losing relevance in today's multi-media digital age. Anthony Paré does not mince words when he asserts that "... changes in the past couple of decades have rendered the single-authored, paper-based, book-length dissertation obsolete" (Paré, 2017, p. 408; Paré, 2019). It may be slowly disappearing, but I do not think it is obsolete yet, whether paper-based or digital, and whether qualitative or quantitative in approach. And of course single-authored monograph-style book publication might follow, post-dissertation.

Doctoral projects and requirements do take multiple forms, of course, including the portfolio approach favored by Paré. The "dissertation (thesis) by publication" and/or the requirement that doctoral students publish in order to graduate is becoming more common in many parts of the world (Lei & Hu, 2015; Li, 2019; Paltridge, 2002), but as Paltridge noted some years ago, is rarely covered thoroughly in the how-to books. This book too, does not do justice to the topic of writing a dissertation (thesis)-by-publication or by means of multi-media productions, but then this is not a how-to-write book. Yes, advice of various kinds appears throughout the book, in some chapters more than in others, but the focus is on helping doctoral students and their supervisors-advisers understand some of the issues that arise during and surrounding writing at the dissertation stage, including the importance of writers' well-being. Regardless of form or of method and approach, the writing of a doctoral dissertation is an enormous high-stakes endeavor that affects many aspects of writers' lives.

Therefore, whether or not doctoral students need to write single-authored monographs or compilations of articles in qualitative, mixed, or quantitative traditions, many matters covered in this book will pertain to all those who are preparing for a final assessment in order to be awarded a doctorate. I refer conventionally to this assessment as involving writing. Regardless of form, the high-stakes doctoral project poses similar challenges to students who are in the midst of writing and challenges as well to their supervisors. Likewise, as a companion to both first (L1) and second or additional (L2) language writers of English, the book bears the message that the challenges that both L1 and L2 writers of English face are similar in that they go beyond language proficiency (Habibie, 2019; Hyland, 2015). In all cases, the topics covered in *During the Dissertation* are ones that arise during writing but that are not usually covered in how-to-write books.

To reiterate, as was the case with *Before the Dissertation*, this book is not designed to teach anyone how to write a doctoral dissertation. Other books exist that try to do this. Books of the start-to-finish type tend to focus on the design and production of text according to typical dissertation or research article templates with chapters or sections devoted to introduction, theoretical framework, literature review, methods, findings/analysis, and discussion-conclusion (the well-known acronym IMRAD—Introduction, Methods, Results, and Discussion—covers most of these). Such how-to books help readers with collection and analysis of data, organizational issues, and linguistic conventions, and presume some uniformity and linearity of writing steps and strategies (see for example Joyner, Rouse, & Glatthorn, 2018; Paltridge & Starfield, 2007, 2019; Swales & Feak, 2012; White, 2011; see also many websites easily located by search engines). Templates offered by such guides may work better for graduate students who are writing quantitative studies rather than the more labor-intensive and less straightforward qualitative or mixed method studies, which by their nature tend to be messier. However, most fully qualitative studies roughly follow similar templates.

Even when the final product follows a predictable template, this says little about how dissertation writers arrived there or what they lived through in the process. Hence, an underlying assumption in *During the Dissertation* is that so much diversity exists in how individuals approach and survive challenging writing tasks like a doctoral dissertation that it is impossible to prescribe, or even suggest, a "best approach." This is the case whether the final doctoral project is a qualitative one or a more predictable quantitative one, or whether it is a monograph or a set of related papers. Moreover, for most doctoral students, writing of many kinds will happen at different stages of the dissertation project, not just post data-collection when the serious drafting begins. Strategies for and timing of these different kinds of writing differ across students, and also across supervisors and advisers who are tasked with helping students complete the dissertation. If dissertation writers do not know by the time they start writing which strategies and issues pertain to them, this book can help them craft some approaches that suit their personalities, preferred practices, and individual goals and visions, and help them figure out how dissertation writing might fit into the real-life intrusions of work and family. Additionally, because actual dissertation writing tends to be a solitary time for L1 and L2 graduate students, a textual mentor like *During the Dissertation* can fill a void in writers' lives at a time of solitude, uncertainty, and anxiety. Keep it under your pillow.

In spite of other kinds of writing and planning that graduate students may have already done, the actual drafting of dissertation chapters or sets of related publishable papers represents a shift of direction and possibly a shift in strategies. In other words, once they have crafted a topic, done some reading, designed the research, collected and analyzed data, and started planning the preliminary writing of the actual draft, dissertation writers begin the real work of writing, revising, and polishing. Unless they are already published book authors, their dissertation writing experience will likely be the first, and perhaps only, time for them to produce such a lengthy and complex work. Many decisions and challenges need to be addressed before actual writing begins, of course, and some of these are covered in the earlier book, *Before the Dissertation*. But at the earliest writing stage, once the preliminary work of design and data collection is done, the challenge for many writers who have not faced such a huge writing project before is to shift attitudes, strategies, and visions of who they are and what they will be doing for the next many months. They need to turn into people who are living the life of writers, not just researchers.

However, if dissertation writers dare to look at other finished dissertations as models (which they are often encouraged to do by well-meaning supervisors), they could become overwhelmed and intimidated to see what lies ahead for them to get to the end point. They may be unable to construct a vision of the whole project and feel they will never be able to produce such a polished and lengthy document, which always looks "perfect," and impossibly long, in its finished form. At this early stage of writing, how can they see themselves as accomplished researchers and writers, whether they are working in their L1 or L2/L3, and so gain the confidence they need in order to move ahead in the actual work of writing and revising? The comparisons are insidious. As useful as it is to look at some finished dissertations, comparisons can potentially be very counterproductive if they lead to self-sabotaging feelings and behaviors. Feeling overly intimidated can result in paralysis and depression at this critical moment of early writing. One message in this book is that it is normal for the dissertation writing experience to be emotional and psychological as well as intellectual. Overly negative feelings therefore need to be understood and managed. The other side of a response to looking at finished dissertations as impossibly perfect is for the dissertation writer to say "I can do this, and I can do it even better." In all cases, it takes courage and tenacity to commit to dissertation writing and to see the process through to the end without being trapped by a belief that perfection is the unreachable goal. Such a belief, instead, needs to be liberating.

I should note from the start that in this book I pay perhaps undue attention to the difficult aspects of and negative responses to doctoral dissertation writing. This strategy makes sense in some ways, because I hope to reach writers who are struggling or dreading or balking or angsting at the dissertation writing stage, and to convince them not to give up, now that they have gotten this far. Dissertation writers who are sailing through their writing probably have little need for this book, beyond curiosity as to what others are going through. It is also likely that dissertation writers will suffer more at the moment of writing than they will recall suffering later. ("I don't know how I'm going to finish/survive this" vs. "It wasn't so bad after all.") I also hope to reach faculty who are advising students on their dissertation writing as a way to alert these advisers and supervisors as to what their students are going through and to remind them what they themselves might have experienced. A little empathy can go a long way.

Nevertheless, let me stress early on that, for many people, the pleasures of doctoral dissertation writing, once a proposal has been accepted, the research has been carried out, and the data have been collected and analyzed, cannot be matched by other experiences in a doctoral program. The writing stage is a time to be totally immersed in one's ideas, goals, challenges, intellectual interests, and writing rituals. It is a deliciously selfish time in this sense, because all attention focuses on YOU, the dissertation writer. A supervisor, classmates with whom students have a supportive relationship such as in a study group, and other faculty are all working together to help dissertation writers get through the writing stage successfully. I should note that students who are reciprocally helping other dissertation writers with their writing also benefit themselves—the comments writers make to others could be comments they are making to themselves.

What, then, are some of the specific issues that arise as dissertation writers immerse themselves in the massively complex job of constructing a book-length piece of research writing or a compilation of related writings for publication, probably for the first time in their lives?

Issues Covered in the Book

In parts of this section, as well as in other places in this book, I address dissertation writers directly rather than referring to them in third person. You, the reader who is currently writing, in addition to general dissertation writers, are my main audience.

To start with, knowing about your own writing styles and strategies when facing a huge and complex project is central from early stages (see Chapter 1), in conjunction with developing a vision of the whole project and its parts (see Chapter 2). Also early on, it is critical to establish a healthy working relationship with supervisors and other faculty and to understand at the writing stage what you and a supervisor expect (see Chapter 3). Some of the studies of doctoral supervising that I refer to in later chapters confirm what dissertation writers know—that not all students have the perfect supervisor-advisee relationship. "Perfect" is taken here to mean a relationship that is low on conflict, high on emotional, intellectual, and procedural engagement and support, and characterized by respect and compatible styles and goals. Neither nagging nor neglect by a supervisor fits into this picture. But perfection in the advising relationship is so rare that dissertation writers need to commit to moving ahead even without it, and if possible, without feeling victimized ("I couldn't finish because my supervisor didn't help me enough....").

It is also helpful to understand ahead of time, as well as at the moments of occurrence, what possible obstacles to writing might confront you. For example, having never done anything like this before, most of us are likely not to know how "perfect" the dissertation needs to be in order to guarantee a successful defense and later, a diploma with our names on it (see Chapter 4). Striving for perfection on such a high-stakes project, as is commonly known, can be very counterproductive by making you feel you need to do more (and more and more and more) and that what you have done so far is never good enough. But as I suggested in the previous paragraph, we may not be able to define what perfection is in dissertation writing. (I think it does not exist.) The compulsion to perfect a dissertation can lead to blocks and burnout, of course, and possible failure to complete the project. Likewise, compulsively following a list of things that other people or guidebooks say you should do can drive your own natural inclinations in counter-productive directions. Yes, it helps to read advice and suggestions from guidebooks and other published and in-person sources (including from this book) about how to get the dissertation written and to make it acceptable, but following prescriptions blindly makes little sense. There are too many "shoulds" out there and not enough focus by writers on their need to continually attend to what works and does not work for them. Pursuing a path suggested by others may turn out not to be productive.

In other words, individual factors greatly influence how you and supervising faculty decide when a dissertation, whatever form it takes, is good enough, if not perfect, and what paths to take to reach this goal. These decisions cannot be made solely from guidebooks or prescriptive advice. Dissertation writers will want to know how good is "good enough," of course, and so you need to keep in touch with supervisors and other critical readers. Otherwise, how do any of us know when to force ourselves to walk away from a document that is not up to our standards or to some imaginary set of standards we think others hold over us or whether we should start over or instead accept the inevitable imperfections? If you stay committed until the end, deadlines imposed by universities will naturally force you to complete the project, even if you feel it is not the model of perfection you had hoped for (ah, the power of deadlines!) (see Chapter 10). Getting through to the end in a timely manner is more likely to require an ongoing awareness of what standards and strategies work for you individually, as well as the tenacity to persist during periods of doubt and confusion. All writers of high-stakes projects need to cultivate this awareness in themselves, and revisit their awareness at different stages of writing.

Addressed minimally in *Before the Dissertation* was the topic of health. In *During the Dissertation* I pay a bit more attention to it because of how important it is to stay healthy in the midst of dissertation writing. Writers who sit at a computer for days and nights (and weeks and months) on end face particular health challenges beyond those of the common cold (see Chapter 5). If you are immersed in a long-term high-stakes project, and are pressed for time as well, you can experience eye strain, joint and muscle problems, fatigue and burnout, poor nutrition, lack of exercise, and all the consequences of these discomforts and poor habits. You risk turning into flabby hunchbacks, junk food and caffeine addicts, pre-diabetics, insomniacs in constant pain, and nervous wrecks who depend on sleeping aids and painkillers to get through long days and possibly short nights. Brain power, in addition to health, suffers. Even if health is basically good, the loneliness and isolation at the writing stage can take a toll on your mental and emotional well-being (see Chapter 7). Dissertation writing is always a challenge, of course, but does not have to be so onerous as to ruin your health.

Nevertheless, even under the best of circumstances, we all have what I call "low- and high-IQ days" (see Chapter 6) and so need to adjust the many different kinds of writing activities to fit such days. Writing does not have to stop on low-IQ days; it just changes to more mechanical tasks. However, on low-IQ days, you may feel more isolated and empty than usual, and wonder if, in the absence of brain power, the mechanical tasks have taken over your lives. I recall asking myself during dissertation writing and even now as I work on other projects: "How long do I have to wait before my brain returns?" It helps, of course, if you can find ways to stay connected to a handful of supportive people to help temper the feeling that you are a solitary imposter who cannot possibly finish this enormous project. A basic source of such support is the school-workplace, where you are likely to have regular contact with other students, colleagues, and co-workers. Even if others cannot make time for in-depth consulting, they can surely assure you that your high-IQ days will indeed return. They can also help you get back on track when you feel isolated and out of touch (see Chapter 7) or overly distracted and beset by interruptions (see Chapter 8).

A major issue for all dissertation writers, those of you with or without a supportive supervisor, is that you all face the generally oppressive task of revising what you have sweat blood and tears to get into a first draft (see Chapter 9). Indeed, all academic writers, and many others who write as well, face the challenging and sometimes tedious task of revising and polishing their work throughout a career. In this small book, I won't review much of the vast literature on correction, feedback, and response to writing, which discusses various ways that writing gets revised and improved (regrettably focusing mainly on corrections to grammar and lexicon, particularly if the advice is given to L2 writers). This literature presumes that someone else, such as a dissertation supervisor, is reading, commenting on, and possibly editing your writing, whether superficially or in great detail.

But supervisors often do not respond in great detail, and instead offer only general comments or even no comments, and may actually refuse to edit and proofread your work. With minimal help from knowledgeable outside readers, how can you move through your revisions without becoming so discouraged that you are ready to give up? To revise successfully, all writers need to cut and paste and toss and keep and shuffle and reorganize and add and expand and then toss some more and finally nit-pick at the punctuation, spelling, spacing, and formatting, having never done this before on a work so large and significant. I hope to convince reluctant revisers that these activities are normal, even as they are sources of anxiety for some of you. I know of only one writer who told me over lunch once, and confirmed it later, that he "loves revising." Really Matt? Maybe you need to write a book on this topic!

And, finally, it will be time to stop (Chapter 10). The difficulty for all academic writers, but especially for dissertation writers, is that we must end a writing project before we feel it is truly finished (as I feel about this book). Even with time extensions in a doctoral program, those extensions will run out and it will be time (as one of my dissertation advisers told me) to either fish or cut bait. We can conclude the project somehow, or we can walk away from it unfinished, after sometimes years of hard work, a regrettable ending but one chosen by about half of all dissertation writers (Golde, 2000, 2005). (See Sternberg's [1981] advice from long ago on reasons for and against writing a doctoral dissertation.) We can understand the temptation to walk away: It can be quite terrifying to imagine ourselves being judged on a high-stakes project before we have perfected the document, but as I discuss in Chapter 4, most of us will never get to the perfection stage. We will inevitably be evaluated on a product that feels unfinished, unperfected, and in need of more revision. We have to stop. It helps to remember that even if you have to finish (meaning submit and defend) before the work feels finished, a new life begins once you can display on your CVs and business cards a new title of "Doctor." And you must not forget that the work can continue, in articles, books, and further research on the dissertation topic and on related and new topics. The search for perfection doesn't need to stop.

Audience for the Book

The primary audience for *During the Dissertation* is L1 (English as a first language) and EAL (English as an Additional Language, also called L2) graduate students who are in the process of writing theses and dissertations in language education fields, although the basic issues apply to dissertation writers in other fields as well. The book is also aimed at interested supervisors and faculty who wish to understand what their advisees are experiencing as these students try to make sense of readings and mounds of data and then selectively put what they can into a book-length piece of writing or compilation of articles. However, many of the struggles that individual students go through are invisible to supervisors, who might see students and their drafts infrequently and who might not feel interested in or responsible for helping students with particular writing problems or with personal struggles. Faculty advisers who read *During the Dissertation* will thus be alerted to what students are going through, and be able to reflect on their own earlier dissertation writing experiences. Such understanding and reflection will help faculty provide first-hand intellectual and emotional support that students might not be able to find in the existing books on "how to write a dissertation." Moreover, supervisors themselves could be experiencing professional and personal stresses that dissertation writers need to be aware of. This book can help all readers do the kind of perspective-taking that will help them better understand the dissertation writing experience from both writers' and supervisors' viewpoints.

Because this book is targeted at both L1 and EAL/L2 graduate students who are writing dissertations in English, it will appeal to domestic graduate students in English dominant countries and to the growing number of international students in graduate programs in these countries (e.g., United States, Canada, United Kingdom, Australia, New Zealand). For L1 users of English, the topics in *During the Dissertation* will likely be both familiar and challenging. For L2 users of English, the chapters deal with issues that they possibly have never confronted in previous academic work and that they may never have discussed openly with supervisors or classmates. Topics that draw on personal struggles and anxieties in academia remain off-bounds in some cultures, as do confessions that a writer needs help and consolation. Such responses should not be seen as signs of weakness in students, but as normal, if hidden, experiences.

Although *During the Dissertation* could easily be used in classes and seminars on dissertation writing, given that each chapter provides rich areas for discussion and for reflective journal writing, the book does not contain extensive discussion questions or activities in the style of some textbooks. A few topics for discussion, journal writing, and reflection stem from the content of the chapters themselves and appear at the end of each chapter. In other words, the book can be used flexibly by individual students as well as by students in seminars and study groups and by their supervisors and faculty, and many chapters can be read individually as needed (hence some repetition across chapters). Even in the midst of intense writing, the goal is for dissertation writers to make time to talk about issues and activities, write about them, and share ideas and concerns so that they are externalized and turned into language that can feed into further writing and reflecting.

Of course, each graduate student who reads this book will likely be at different stages of the dissertation writing process, and be facing different sorts of personal and intellectual challenges. Every reader will thus benefit from some chapters more than others. I urge all readers therefore to study the Table of Contents, and then to pick and choose what to read, when to read, and even how to read (such as with care and attention, or with a goal of a quick overview). I also urge those dissertation writers who are not already doing so to keep a reflective journal as they read this and any other resources, and also as they write. In some cases, excerpts from this kind of journal writing might also end up in the dissertation itself or in post-dissertation writing, so it is not wasted time to do this kind of reflective writing. My own journal-like excerpts and commentaries that might parallel writers' own journal reflections appear throughout the book. Many additions can be made to the commentaries in *During the Dissertation* from each reader's experiences, including issues I have not included or dealt with in enough detail or looked at from enough perspectives. So let's get started.

Chapter 1

Where to Start?

How can I finish if I never start?

This introductory chapter asks doctoral dissertation writers to get to know themselves and their strategies for writing complex high-stakes academic work early in the dissertation writing process. Once writers know themselves and their strategies, they can monitor and adjust what they do from proposal writing to writing the full dissertation. Included are discussions on loving and hating one's writing and writing projects, maintaining a clear sense of purpose for doing a dissertation, anticipating moments of both order and chaos, finding the best times and places to write, and cultivating a flexible and tenacious outlook.

Getting Started on "Where to Start"

I had to smile at myself as I began writing this chapter because I am facing the same challenge that I write about, namely, where to start. Reading about where to start writing up a big project, and then how to finish it (see, for example, Becker's wonderful old book from 1986 on how to start and finish your thesis) doesn't help much when it comes to actually doing the work. The "how-to" books somehow make it all look too easy (see some references in Chapter 2). But some parts of the writing are easier than others. In other projects, and in my consultations with doctoral students, I sometimes advise myself and students to do the easy stuff first, which usually means not starting at the beginning, but somewhere in the middle. Besides, as Annie Dillard (1989, p. 5) reminded us, "It is the beginning of a work that the writer throws away" and has to do over. This is particularly true for doctoral dissertation writing, given that some of the middle parts of the project are well understood and fleshed out before the writing begins, such as profiles of participants and descriptions of research sites or methods and procedures. Once dissertation researchers have chosen a site and participants, they can describe these relatively easily, without struggling over theoretical or analytical issues. Similarly, a methods chapter is often easier to write early in the writing process than other chapters of a dissertation, because it is usually presented as a straightforward description of what the researchers did and how they did it. Also, much of the methods chapter probably has already been written in the dissertation proposal. The writer then just needs to change "I will do xyz" to "I did xyz" and adjust details as needed. In short, start with what is easiest, I hear myself telling students, particularly if you are second language writers of English. Getting some writing done early and getting comfortable with terminology for your topic will boost your confidence and give you a sense of what kinds of language help you might need later.

Other parts of a dissertation are almost impossible to write at early stages of drafting, although some of the more difficult sections, such as a framework and a literature review, have been drafted for the proposal, even if they get changed later. For instance, even though it is tempting to begin at the beginning, the full introduction chapter is not a great place to begin, because so many things might change during the actual dissertation writing. It is sometimes best to write, or at least to finish, the introduction chapter last, when an honest and accurate overview of the project can be described (see a bit more on this strategy in Chapter 2).

But here I am, starting my writing of this book with Chapter 1, and not only that, but at the beginning of Chapter 1. I can justify this choice by pointing out first that I have already sketched out the structure and contents of the entire book, so I can begin about anywhere the muse strikes me. Second, unlike chapters in a dissertation, the chapters in this book can pretty much stand alone. It is therefore not so tempting to think I need to begin at the beginning and proceed in order through a prescribed structure. Third, one way that I often ease myself into a major writing task is to begin with an anecdote such as the one I start with here—a bit of personal connection to a topic that describes how I started the writing. Of course, I could do that with any chapter. But fourth, I am living right now what I need to write about in this chapter—where to start the actual writing of a major project. If you feel blocked, why not start with a personal connection? The point is to start anywhere you can, in any chapter, beginning, middle, or end. Getting any chunk of writing done will give you a sense of accomplishment that can inspire further writing sessions.

Having said all this, I must also say that it is crucial to know (and continue learning about) yourself as a writer. If you are an L2 writer of English, this includes knowing your writing strategies and challenges in your L1. There may be useful parallels and comparisons to be made between your L1 and L2 writing strategies. However, many L2 dissertation writers I have known have done little or no academic writing in their L1s, having completed their graduate level academic work at English-dominant universities. If you are one of these, forge ahead and work directly in

English, and learn about the strategies for writing in English that have or have not worked for you in the past. Knowing something about yourself as a writer of English includes recognizing whether you are tempted to write first in your L1 and then translate. At this advanced level of writing, please don't write by translation! Translating is a skill and art of its own, not the same as composing. It may help lower level learners learn the language, but without helping them learn how to write (Kobayashi & Rinnert, 1992), and may also help L2 writers at the planning stages of writing, when "thinking" often happens in the L1 (Tavakoli, Ghadiri, & Zabihi, 2014). Yet even intermediate level L2 writers may do better writing directly in their L2, as Cohen and Carson-Brooks (2001) found some time ago in their study of French learners. L2 dissertation writers are, of course, way beyond intermediate levels of proficiency.

In other words, whether you are an L1 or an L2 writer, it is important to assess early on what you know, or still need to learn, about writing strategies that work for you, the topics you will be writing about, and any specialized language associated with your topics. Only by knowing yourself as a writer will you be able to follow, resist, or alter the suggestions in this book or in any other writing guide, or from supervisors and faculty and peers who may be helping you manage your dissertation writing. This includes knowing about yourself as a writer of different kinds of texts in whatever languages you use in academic contexts. Let me explore this point a bit further.

Knowing Yourself as a Writer

All writers who know their strengths, weaknesses, and strategies for writing before starting any major writing project are miles, kilometers, or possibly light years ahead of those who do not. Such writers know what ups and downs to expect; they can guess what might come easily and what will be difficult; they can anticipate which strategies to use if obstacles arise; they know when the best times of day are to write. In other words, they can use their knowledge of themselves as writers to get something done even on days when their goals seem out of reach, when their brains are full of mush, or when precious stretches of uninterrupted writing time are rare. When they feel stalled or pressured by impossible deadlines, they recognize that swelling feeling of mild panic that begins somewhere in the stomach and travels mercilessly up to the chest and then to the brain, and they know some steps to take in order to quell the anxiety. They know when it is hopeless for them to try to write, and so use such moments to do other things that can contribute eventually to a better writing session, like getting some sleep or some exercise, both essential for good brain functioning.

One of the most useful activities I have found at times when my writing seems to be blocked, in addition to rereading my own previous drafts, is to go back to some reading that is related to the writing I need to do, particularly a reading that I have enjoyed for its ideas or for its quality of writing. The activity of (re)reading is usually pleasurable, and it can take the pressure off needing to write, and at the same time can fold our thoughts back into the writing that awaits us. Beware of using reading as an escape mechanism, however. It is so easy to convince oneself that it is not possible to start or continue writing because we have not read enough. With this kind of reasoning, we will never be able to start a day's writing session.

Another activity that can help turn a bad writing day into at least a marginally productive session is to do needed mechanical work. For instance, compile references, format them into the style that is required, and proofread them. Such work might involve preparing items for a bibliographic software application or compiling them "by hand." Whatever system you use, building a master list of bibliographic references that can be added to over time will serve you throughout your academic careers. And if you haven't done this already, why not also make a copy of the references in list or table form in which you copy and paste abstracts or summaries of the readings as a handy reminder of what you have read? If your brain empties out as quickly as mine does, you'll appreciate the resources that result from such mechanical work later. This kind of mechanical work is usually done early in the dissertation project, of course, rather than in the midst of writing, but can usefully continue at various stages of writing. Managing your readings at times when you feel stuck will give you a sense of accomplishment and also provide useful resources and memory triggers for later (see Wikipedia for a comparison of some bibliographic software applications: https://en.wikipedia.org/wiki/Comparison_of_reference_management_software).

In general, for all of us, getting to know ourselves as writers involves paying attention to what worked or did not work in the past as we engaged in different kinds of writing. What kinds of writing led to a smooth and fluent outpouring of language (Csikszentmihalyi, 1996)? Why was writing relatively effortless in such cases? It often seems associated with thorough topic knowledge and a clear sense of purpose, and is such a pleasure when it happens! In contrast, what kinds of writing or writing sessions left us struggling to pull even short phrases or a single inspired idea out of our tortured brains? What made such writing so difficult? The reasons may be due only partially to insufficient topic knowledge. Clearly, in both cases no single answer will do justice to the complexity of what writing means to each individual, but it will help to ask the questions and to pay attention to the details of past and present writing experiences. These are great questions to discuss with colleagues and classmates who are also in the midst of writing, by the way, and can be the source of some good-humored confessions and comparisons as you learn more about yourself and others as writers.

Loving and Hating Writing

Some questions about knowing ourselves as writers are more basic than others. One place I like to start with dissertation writers I have worked with is to find out whether they love or hate to write. In some cases, the response will be clear and swift—someone who has always hated to write will generally not start loving it come dissertation time. Someone who has always loved to write, or at least not had an antagonistic relationship with writing, will also be able to respond quickly and positively to the early stages of dissertation writing. But most of us will probably respond with "it depends." For instance, I rather enjoy writing when I am writing something by choice rather than by obligation; when I am writing about a topic I enjoy and know something about already; when deadlines are present but not too pressing; and when I have had sufficient sleep.

If you are a dissertation writer who belongs to this "it depends" group, you need to figure out what precisely your responses depend on to doing different kinds of writing. I recall more than one doctoral student telling me, for example, that they could not write academic texts in their native language (Japanese), only in English. After my initial surprise, this made some sense—all their reading and writing and much of their discussion in their American university masters and doctoral programs had been done in English. Also, they had not ever written or read major academic texts in their native language related to their dissertation topics, if such texts even existed, and may not have had much graduate level writing experience at all in Japanese. It is worth paying attention to past experiences with and attitudes toward writing academic texts in an L1 or L2, because the knowledge can be used productively to help you manage future writing.

For those students and scholars who love to write (yes, there are a few), whether in L1 or L2, words and sentences and paragraphs may come relatively easily, depending on which part of the dissertation or other projects you are working on. Many of us are envious of such writers, but it is one thing to love to write and another to be in love with your own writing. It can be dangerous to be too much in love with your own writing because the revising and pruning become so difficult. I recall Annie Dillard (1989) writing about composing a perfect sentence, after much difficulty, and then being forced to cut it because it just did not belong. It is difficult to throw away chunks of work that have taken days or weeks to compose, particularly if you feel that the passages are brilliant. This is why it is comforting to transfer such chunks to a "garbage" file that will not actually be thrown away (see the section in Chapter 9 on learning to love the garbage bin). The brilliant bits can always be mined later, in future work. It is only a little easier to prune if the writer who loves writing ends up hating what has taken so much effort to compose. But dissertations, and academic journal articles as well, pose word and length limits on writers. Pruning and cutting are inevitable. Even so, when a supervisor or a manuscript reviewer or journal editor tells you that you must reduce a section or chapter or article by a third, the task can seem impossible, particularly if you love the parts that must be cut.

On the other hand, if you are a dissertation writer who hates to write, or hates certain kinds of writing, including your own, being in a doctoral program puts you in a bit of a pickle. In a doctoral program and a career in the social sciences, writing is what people do, particularly in fields such as education and many subfields of applied linguistics, where writing is a way of life. Also, more and more doctoral programs around the world are requiring that students write for publication to graduate. Whatever the doctoral program, once the normally pleasurable activities of reading and collecting and analyzing data are completed, you are stuck with having to write and to critically review and revise your own writing (difficult to do if you hate your own writing!). It can be tempting to flee at this point, which many students do, leaving a doctoral program ABD—All But Dissertation (see the brief discussion in Chapter 8, and Sternberg's 1981 book, devoted entirely to helping ABDs finish their dissertations). Attrition rates in doctoral programs around the world are high and the reasons numerous (Council of Graduate Schools, 2019; Farkas, 2018; Gardner, 2008; Golde, 2000, 2005; Lovitts, 2001; Lovitts & Nelson, 2000). We can only hope that the need or desire to complete the doctoral degree is a stronger motivator than hating to write and hating what you have written is a de-motivator.

In short, as Dillard said more colorfully than I have, both loving and hating your writing excessively are counter-productive: "The feeling that the work is magnificent, and the feeling that it is abominable, are both mosquitoes to be repelled, ignored, or killed, but not indulged" (p. 15).

Starting with and Maintaining a Sense of Purpose

Obviously, the main purpose of dissertation writing is to finish the project and get a doctoral degree. However, I think this purpose alone is insufficient for many dissertation writers—it is simply too instrumental. Especially difficult to sustain are projects that are done and written by a solitary individual, as is often the case for dissertation writers in the soft disciplines, if there are no other long-term purposes that have some intrinsic value for the dissertation writer. Co-authored project work can fruitfully be pursued later, but at the dissertation stage, novice scholars are pretty much on their own. This is why, as I discussed in *Before the Dissertation*, choice of topic is so central to maintaining a sense of purpose in a long-term difficult project. I am the voice of experience here—I lost one year of dissertation progress by starting with a topic that I could not sustain and that did not sustain my interest. I had to start over.

A sustaining sense of purpose is driven mainly by both need and want. Someone who needs a doctoral degree in order to get or keep a job will be instrumentally motivated to start and then finish even if a topic is not compelling. This instrumental sense of purpose will likely get us through, but we might not have much fun. A more compelling sense of purpose stems from intrinsic interest in a topic, one that is complex enough to last for all the dissertation years and beyond without driving us crazy with boredom. The questions and curiosities need to be both genuine to the writer and ones that have no easy answers, or even better, no certain answers at all. Uncertainty can lead to further research once the dissertation is completed. A sense of purpose is also driven by a vision of the whole, of the end product (see Chapter 2), and of life after the dissertation. Within this sustaining sense of purpose will be mini-steps of course—small goals to be accomplished week to week and month to month, possibly enshrined in lists whose items can be crossed off, with great pleasure, as they are accomplished. These interim goals align with and are subsumed under the overall purpose. In all cases you can both start with and renew your sense of purpose by regularly asking "Why am I doing this project? Why is it important to me and to others?"

Relishing the Order and Tolerating (if Not Embracing) the Chaos

By the time you have completed a proposal, collected data, and started to produce drafts of your dissertation, you are likely to have a sense of order in your data and analytic schemes, and maybe even have a good outline of some or all of the dissertation you will be writing. I assume, without experience to back this up, that students who have done an experimental or a survey study have inherently more order in their projects from the start than do people like me, who are drawn to the messiness of qualitative projects. But even qualitative researchers can benefit from a systematic, ordered approach to their data, analysis, and writing, so that getting started at drafting is somehow not so tortured as it is for some of us who cannot even put together an outline of what we will write. If it is clear from the start what needs to be written, writing sessions might be tedious at times, but will not leave you struggling to figure out how or where to begin or continue a draft. I recall interviewing a well-published senior professor of sociology once, a participant in the project for my own dissertation, about how he went about his writing, which was based mostly on quantitative survey research. He said it was quite easy: He wrote a detailed outline, down to the paragraph level, and then just filled in the blanks, paragraph by paragraph. I can only read and dream about such order, or listen to stories of people who are more orderly in their approaches than I have ever been. (I am not sure why I have never been able to construct outlines before I begin writing. A "don't fence me in" mentality? Or a belief that creativity and insights can happen in the midst of unstructured writing? Or just a selectively disordered mind?)

If it is normal for the writers of quantitative survey and experimental work to both relish and benefit from an orderly approach to writing from the very start of a project, it is also advisable for others, in the views of some, to pursue orderly writing strategies to the extent possible. If one is to believe Creswell (2016), qualitative researchers also profit from order and systematicity in their data collection, analysis, and writing. I read Creswell's book with interest, in spite of my general skepticism about how-to books. I found that most of his "30 essential skills" for qualitative researchers involve making order: creating tables with a lot of neatly labeled columns and rows; identifying codes in data; combining codes into themes; using themes as main headings and subheadings of the dissertation; and so on. Creswell made the writing seem relatively painless once all this order has been made. Writers know where to start, what to say, and what order to say it in. I have never been able to make this kind of detailed, concrete, and visible order before I begin writing, and am envious of those who can, even though I thrive on "to-do" lists. Still, I manage somehow to finish writing projects now and then, so others certainly can, too. If order is not present at the start of a project, it will get imposed later.

Those of us with somewhat unsystematic minds and working habits must learn to embrace the chaos of a major writing project like a dissertation, particularly one that follows a qualitative approach, and find other, less concrete ways to make order as we write. Before I can construct anything even as basic as a list of topics, or if I am struggling with a particularly difficult section of writing, I mull, particularly as I walk, which I do every day. Even my reading is interrupted by mulling, which is one reason I cannot get through my reading very fast. The mulling feels quite chaotic and inefficient, and I am never sure where it will lead. Sometimes ideas and order for a project come to me quickly, holistically, as a vision of the whole (again, see Chapter 2), after many days of mulling. If I am blessed with a vision of the whole, the writing can start fairly easily, but usually this process is slow and halting. Although I feel I know myself as a writer, I do not know how to make the process of chaos-to-mulling-to-vision-to-writing happen faster, or even happen at all. I can only allow myself the time and space to read, to ponder, and occasionally to get my face out of the computer screen, whose relentless glow constantly reminds me what I have yet to do. Strict deadlines help of course, but they can also stifle creativity and contribute to paralysis in productivity.

However, like some others who write about people in their research, I find that thinking narratively can help make order out of chaos (Barkhuizen, 2013, 2014; Clandinin, 2007; Riessman, 2008). As has often been said, lives are storied (Bruner, 1991), and in writing about people for dissertations and other major projects it is possible to think in terms of making order through narratives as we begin to write. The dissertation, after all, is itself a kind of story, with a beginning, middle, and end, whose parts must cohere. There are characters, settings, plots that contain twists and turns, and resolutions, even in people's messy lives. Starting with stories in mind can reduce the anxiety we feel from chaos.

Finding the Right Times and Places to Write

Possibly all dissertation writers know enough about themselves as writers to know when the best times of the day are for them to write, and where the best locations are as well (see more on *space* and *place* in Chapter 8). If not, it makes sense early in a writing project as large as a dissertation to identify the times and places that are most conducive to writing. Sometimes these choices are beyond your control: Jobs, family responsibilities, and constrained living quarters can dictate when and where people write. One of my doctoral students had two children during the years she was supposed to be working on her dissertation. I recently re-read the several years of email we exchanged during this entire time, and felt quite overwhelmed at her tales of trying to find time, energy, and quiet places to concentrate, particularly when she was sleep-deprived. I still don't know how she did it, but she identified times and places that would work for her at the earliest stages of writing, and changed them as needed during those years when children transform from infancy into creatures with whom one can have a conversation.

Drawing on Annie Dillard's *The Writing Life* (1989) again, I was intrigued at the many descriptions Dillard included of her places to write: cabins in the woods, studios, and beach hideaways. But I have to disagree with her assertion that "Appealing workplaces are to be avoided." "One wants a room with no view," she continued, "so imagination can meet memory in the dark" (p. 26). She thus blocked off the windows in her cabins. I, in contrast, cannot imagine writing without plenty of natural light and windows around me. I can touch-type without looking steadily at a keyboard, so spend some of my writing time looking out the big picture window in the library, even though my mind and fingers are immersed in the writing. I have tried to write at home (my house is quiet, comfortable), but I don't seem to be able to do this easily. Hence my forays to the school library, at rather predictable times of the day, where I am not distracted by all the things that a home environment can distract me with. I also cannot write in the early morning, or at night. I must compress my writing time into late mornings and afternoons. Knowing this, my writing time is more efficient than if I persisted in trying to write at times and in places that do not suit me. Helen Sword (2017) learned that successful academics write in so many different places and at so many different times of day that advice cannot be given that fits everyone. The point is that whenever and wherever you write, make adjustments, if possible, if times and places are not working for you.

Staying Flexible and Tenacious

Finally, it is a good idea for dissertation writers and other writers including me to begin a writing project by committing to a stance that is both flexible and tenacious in how we write and how we think about our writing. If nothing is fixed in stone, then there are no right and wrong ways to go about our writing tasks, in spite of what the how-to books might recommend (see advice in Badenhorst, & Guerin, 2016b; Becker, 1986; Bitchener, 2010, 2017; Creswell, 2016; Glatthorn, Rouse, & Joyner, 2013; Joyner, Rouse, & Glatthorn, 2018; Paltridge & Starfield, 2007, 2019, among others). We can experiment and adjust and revise continuously, so there is no need for any of us to feel anxious as we start to write. This means we also need to tenaciously keep moving ahead so that our writing styles and strategies can accommodate the changes, bumps in the road, gaps in knowledge, dips in confidence and energy, and the ongoing learning that a major writing project like a dissertation is certain to provide us.

But it is impossible to move ahead with first getting started.

SUMMARY OF MAIN POINTS

1. Strategies for getting started on dissertation writing vary so much by individual that it is difficult to predict or describe what might work best for each dissertation writer.
2. Knowing yourself as a writer is essential for crafting what writing strategies will work best.
3. Writers who either love or hate writing will find different approaches for getting started, but all dissertation writers need to maintain a sense of purpose and flexibility.

SUGGESTIONS FOR DISCUSSION AND REFLECTION

1. In general, do you enjoy or dislike writing? Does your response depend on the kinds of writing you do?
2. Once you have done some reading and collected some data, do you find it difficult or easy to get started on the actual writing of a major project like a dissertation? What makes the early writing easy or difficult?
3. What different writing tasks do you do on days when you find writing easy or difficult? How do you try to get yourself writing if you feel stalled?

Chapter 2

Vision of the Whole/ Vision of the Parts

Is a doctoral dissertation a jigsaw puzzle or a canvas?

This chapter begins with some reflections on writing a dissertation proposal (also referred to as a prospectus in some literature), and how a well-done proposal, along with a good title, establishes a vision of an entire project. The proposal actually includes a great deal of writing that is likely to remain in the finished dissertation, even if changes are made, so it is appropriate to discuss it even briefly for this book (see also *Before the Dissertation*). With a good proposal, envisioning the parts of the whole dissertation can help writers break down the writing into manageable pieces. Each of the individual chapters (called "part-genres" by some; Bitchener, 2017; Bitchener, Basturkmen, & East, 2010) and subsections within typical chapters can be worked on separately, and later compiled and fit together as one would a jigsaw puzzle. This sounds deceptively easy phrased this way, however. Even when all the parts are drafted, the whole needs to look like a whole—like a finished canvas—not like a fragmented collection of jigsaw-puzzle parts. Hence the need for the larger vision.

Initial Musings

For some people, a vision of the whole doctoral dissertation (or master's thesis, or even book) begins before any writing at all has taken place. This initial vision might not involve anything in writing at all, but I still refer to it as "writing." It comes to the mind and body while the writer is on a walk, in the shower, on a solitary drive, or in the half-conscious moments before sleeping or waking. I am one of those to whom this happens sometimes, as I described briefly in Chapter 1. The vision might come to me in the form of a title, that, if I am lucky, guides the entire project (discussed in more detail later). When the vision of a whole project descends on me, embodied in a title or as a more complex vision, it usually happens on a solitary walk after I have been reading and thinking for many months. My subconscious has fodder upon which to feed. Other people who lack an initial guiding title or vision will need to slog through multiple drafts of notes and outlines, forcing order onto bits and pieces of ideas and intuitions, or instead to adopt a vision prepared by someone else, such as that of the principle faculty investigator of a research team or a dissertation supervisor. By whatever means it happens, a vision of the whole is worth cultivating early in the dissertation writing process, and can feed directly into the first real writing that dissertation writers do—the proposal to conduct dissertation research. Even without any concrete research results, and often even without any data, the proposal is the initial written vision of the whole, and often becomes part of the full dissertation.

For programs that require a formal proposal, the work required to prepare, draft, and revise this important document can take a year or more. (And sometimes the unfortunate proposal writer has to start over, if one idea for a proposal doesn't work out, as happened to me and that I mentioned in Chapter 1 and described in *Before the Dissertation*.) Programs such as those in the United States that require several years of course work in addition to a formal proposal can deceive you into waiting until course work is done to begin working on a proposal. Bad idea. Such a linear approach does not take advantage of the growth and dovetailing and merging of ideas that can happen if you begin to think about your dissertation projects early in the program, not only about the content, but also the formal requirements and departmental expectations. Course work and the associated readings, if selected and attended to carefully, can inspire many ideas for a dissertation. In all cases, students who are preparing a proposal need to do vast amounts of reading and thinking at various points before and during proposal writing, but without letting the reading rob you of your own fresh ideas. You will benefit as well from discussions with others who are experienced in proposal and dissertation writing—more senior classmates, advisers, graduates, other faculty, but also with others who are just beginning to write. For those students and supervisors who like a how-to approach, books and articles can provide advice and sometimes ready-made how-to templates (Becker, 1986; Joyner, Rouse, & Glatthorn, 2018; Kamler & Thomson, 2014; Kilbourn, 2006; Krathwohl, & Smith, 2005; Locke, Spirduso, & Silverman, 2017; Mewburn, 2019a, 2019b; Murray & Beglar, 2009; Rockquemore, 2016; Paltridge & Starfield, 2019; Sternberg, 1981), but beware of taking these on uncritically.

I often tell doctoral students that once they have written a good proposal, they have actually written about one-third of their dissertations. Even if adjustments are made later, once the proposal is done, you have managed to draft the dissertation's introduction and rationale, to lay out conceptual or theoretical frameworks, to begin or nearly finish literature reviews, to pose the inquiry questions and curiosities, and to describe procedures in a methods chapter. In other words, the proposal lays out the vision of the whole project, provides the grounding in existing literature, identifies contexts and participants, and articulates how the project will get done. Perhaps not all doctoral programs require such a detailed proposal, but sketchier proposals still ask dissertation writers to construct an overall plan for the project. This vision of the whole can guide the project over months and even years and offer you a sense of security when the parts are being fleshed out and when writing processes seem chaotic and messy.

The vision of the whole can be quite intimidating, of course. In contrast, envisioning the parts that fit within the whole, and then envisioning the sub-(sub-)parts that fit within the parts, can help dissertation writers focus on small pieces of the project without feeling overwhelmed by the larger vision. As I write this, I realize that I might be talking about a kind of outlining—a practice I have never done and, for reasons I don't fully understand, cannot make myself do. The "vision of the whole/vision of the parts" perspective accomplishes some of the same things that an outline does, but does not feel so formal or fixed (constraining?) to me. As I planned this book, for instance, I began with an overall vision of what I wanted to accomplish, and then made a list of possible chapter topics, refining and rearranging those over weeks as I considered some of the specific themes that would fit within the whole book. The first and last chapters were easy to place—Where to Start, and Time to Stop. But other chapter topics got added, tossed, merged, expanded, and sorted, at which point I developed short descriptive blurbs for each one. At that point, I could put all chapters out of my mind but for the one I was working on. In a sense, the vision of the whole permitted me to identify and work on the parts, and reduce the potentially intrusive and intimidating larger vision, which nevertheless remained in the background, lurking relentlessly, and guiding the whole project.

Dissertation chapters are much more predictable than the chapters in a book like this one, of course. Many dissertations follow a template-like structure, whether they adopt a qualitative, quantitative, or mixed method paradigm. The conventional structure for dissertations and journal articles —Introduction, Methods, Results-Analysis, Discussion and Conclusion (IMRAD; see Preface)—written about in the field of applied linguistics by John Swales (2004; Swales & Feak, 2012) and others (Cheng, 2018; Paltridge & Starfield, 2007) is a testament to the predictability of these academic genres. I must note, however, that the IMRAD acronym nevertheless does not describe or prescribe separate chapters or sections on theoretical frameworks and literature reviews that are needed in some dissertations. Perhaps the work done by the framework and literature review sections will fit into an introductory chapter. However, in the dissertation templates I am familiar with, theoretical frameworks and literature reviews form separate chapters or sections that distinguish conceptual from empirical work.

Regardless of the guiding structure, each main chapter features sections and subsections that can be addressed by dissertation writers in manageable chunks or "part-genres." For my own qualitative dissertation, I lacked an initial vision of the whole beyond a very broad early curiosity about writing in the disciplines and how it helped shape identities. Still, I followed the dissertation template. I wrote the conventional first three chapters for my proposal (Introduction, Conceptual Framework and Literature Review, Methods), then later constructed three main chapter themes for my findings. Perhaps each of the findings chapters functioned as a kind of guiding thematic vision that allowed me within those chapters to discuss each of my case study participants individually. I was able to work on one chapter and one participant at a time without being distracted by the other pieces. However, my conceptual framework was written separately as part of my proposal, and I am embarrassed to confess in retrospect probably was not linked closely enough to my main research topic. I did not have a good vision of the whole at that time into which the conceptual chapter could fit, but could not let go of some of the interesting readings I had done even though they might not have been particularly relevant. Somehow the chapter survived. I also did not have dissertation advisers, as effective as they were in other ways, who guided me to think in terms of a whole-part vision. The result was, unrecognized by me at the time, that the whole did not hang together as well as it could have.

I wonder now if it is even possible to have a clear vision of the whole at the start of a dissertation project. It is no doubt challenging for dissertation writers who might still be novice scholars to develop a vision of the whole at early stages of writing. Do they, and did I, have the grounding needed to construct such a guiding vision, in particular one that is feasible for a dissertation project? Up until actual dissertation writing, most of us write only course papers. How much do we have to know in order to develop a vision of a very large whole at such early stages? Even if such a vision is incomplete or flawed, I think it is still worth trying to construct it. With an overall vision in place, writers are able to imagine the pieces that go into its construction, to select small pieces to work on even at the paragraph level, and to begin a day's work at any location they want in the whole project. They can later go back to these small parts after the pieces are crafted and weave them together into the whole, adjusting and revising as needed.

Whatever approaches you use in the whole-part construction of your work, the actual dissertation writing does not typically happen as a linear process beginning with the introduction chapter (often finished last) and proceeding to the conclusion. Instead, it is a piecemeal activity that happens within the overall vision. Each small part that gets written, and not tossed, will eventually find its way into the whole. I turn now to a discussion of some of the conventional parts of a dissertation, not as a how-to guide, but as more of a conceptual look at how to think about each part and its contribution to the whole. I am not presenting these sections in the usual order found in how-to books that begin with the introduction and proceed through different stages to the conclusion and implications, but in an order in which you as a dissertation writer might actually work on these parts.

Titles

Titles can be created first, last, or in the middle of a dissertation project and can always be changed. But a good title, created at the beginning a project, can guide the project, from beginning to end (Creswell, 2015). It encapsulates the whole vision and functions as a cognitive organizer. A good title is clear and substantive, even catchy, without being overly clever. Even though a good title is short (ideally 10 words or fewer), it identifies the topic, participants, methodological approach, and research site (Creswell, 2016). It might consist of one phrase, or a main phrase followed by a subtitle after a colon (very common). I suggest doing as many versions of a dissertation title as needed, up until the final draft is being revised and polished, and to make it clear enough for a key word search to locate it easily on a database. Try to indicate what, who, how, and where in as efficient a way as possible. If your title could be that of a 10-volume series on a topic, it is too broad. If it specifies so many details that it requires three or four lines on the title page, it is too narrow. If your classmates and colleagues can't figure out from your title what you are writing about, it is too vague or obscure. Do any of these titles (all invented) work for you?

1. "Academic Writing and Undergraduate Students"
2. "Learning to Write Academic Essays, Reports, Articles, Blogs, and Book Reviews: An Exploration into the Social, Psychological, Intellectual, Cultural, Political, and Historical Foundations of Academic Literacy Development in the Lives of Fourteen Undergraduate International Students from China in an English Language Bachelor's Degree Program in the South-Central Region of the Midwestern United States"
3. "Postmodern Translingualism and Hypernormativity in Academic Literacy: Reenactments of Angst among Post-Secondary Youth"

Ok, I exaggerate, but you get my point. Don't write titles like these.

Reading for the Dissertation Project

It is likely that much of the reading that dissertation writers do happens at the planning and proposal stages. This makes a great deal of sense, because reading can help you develop a vision of the whole. Also, early in-depth reading makes sense because it is impossible to read intensively and write intensively at the same time. (If any readers out there can do this, please write a book or article on how!) I also find it impossible to plan and then write a major academic project without knowing something about what has already been done on my topic and about how projects have been carried out. In Chapter 5 of *Before the Dissertation*, I addressed some of the issues, citing Becky Kwan's (2008, 2009) work among other sources, so I won't repeat them in detail here. I'll just say that in that chapter, I discussed my view that it is important to read early in a project, but also gave counter-views, such as those long ago of sociologist Robert Merton (1967) and anthropologist Harry Wolcott (2001), who believed that reading early in a project can stifle one's own thinking. In Wolcott's view, it is writing, not reading, that helps scholars focus their thinking. I also discussed the problems of finding, selecting, and evaluating readings, a nearly impossible task to do well and efficiently when one is a novice scholar. We all need help doing this. For most of us, reading of some kind continues throughout a major project up until the most intensive writing stage, at which point we find it difficult to stop reading. A common feeling is that we cannot really start writing, and certainly not finish it, because we don't know enough yet. But we will never know enough. We have to stop reading, at least temporarily.

So I will just say that for any large writing project, I and dissertation writers I have worked with have found the reading period to be both pleasurable and frustrating. It is pleasurable because it is a time of expansive learning that can feed into a vision of the whole. Readers come to know the topics, issues, and main contributors in a field, and can usefully write about them in response journals, research memos, and early drafts of the dissertation proposal, and discuss them with colleagues along the way. Readers can also draw on the help of more experienced scholars so that precious time is not wasted on materials that are clearly irrelevant. However, it is not always possible to know what sources are and are not relevant early in a project, even if one is a fairly experienced scholar, hence the frustration of searching for and assessing materials. Likewise, many faculty advisers are not specialists in dissertation writers' particular topics, and will not have read everything (anything?) that writers need to read. My own advisers, competent as they were, did not know anything about L2 writing, but they could guide me in how to do research and help me find relevant L1 sources on academic and disciplinary literacy. It can come as a surprise to some dissertation writers that their adviser does not know everything.

A further pleasure, on the other hand, is getting to know the names, views, and writing styles of the authors one is reading, and eventually reaching the saturation point, where the author names and ideas become familiar. At this point, you are likely to be more of an expert in your particular topic than is your adviser, a confidence-booster if there ever was one. The frustrating side of this stage is that it is tempting to continue reading the authors and topics that you are becoming familiar with, even in the midst of writing, when more reading might not actually contribute to the dissertation. I found that it was very difficult to stop reading for my dissertation and to start writing for real. Arthur Applebee (R.I.P.), low-keyed and taciturn as always, had to sit me down and tell me: "Chris, stop reading." His exact words.

Whatever systems you have for reading and whether you read early, mid, or late in the dissertation writing process or throughout the entire writing time (possible but unlikely), keep track of everything in a way that allows you to find what you need later—in reading response journals, bibliographic lists, tables, information management systems such as Endnote if you are so inclined, and so on (Casanave, 2011, 2014). If you begin with a system that doesn't seem to be working for you, then change it. One doctoral student I know devised a very handy and systematic table, with columns and rows, for reading items and for several categories of comments. However, he found after not too long that this system was simply taking too much time to write. Another student tried using Endnote to keep track of citations and references, essential to do during writing, and found it resulted in more mistakes than he could handle. He said:

> So, I have learned a valuable lesson. Endnote and some of the citation generators are sneaky and not to be trusted. Holy cow that was a minefield. When combined with some of the previous edits and miscellaneous moving of pieces, there were an awful lot of broken/missing sources. (Scott S., January 28, 2018)

In short, find or make your own system for keeping track of and writing about readings, and adjust it if it is not working well for you. The readings will be central in helping you develop your vision of the whole.

Writing about What You Did

From one perspective, it makes sense to start the actual dissertation writing by writing drafts of a literature review, particularly if you have done quite a bit of reading early on and organized it in some way that makes it easy to find what you need. However, writing a literature review is very difficult, as I comment on in the next section. A boost in motivation and confidence can come if the early stages of actual writing are easier, hence my suggestion to my own doctoral students to begin with the methods chapter. The methods chapter is a required element at the proposal stage that can usually be transported directly into the full dissertation. Usually some fleshing out, minor adjustments, and a simple tense change are all that is required later to describe what you did rather than what you will do, but other changes can be made as needed. And by describing what you did, whom you did it with, and where, you have described in some sense the whole of your project.

Here is what one student wrote to me:

> I remember you gave me good advice that I can start from writing methods. It is not as intimidating as writing a lit review because you are simply explaining the process. Also, knowing whatever I wrote in the proposal is not a final product was a relief. (Mayumi Asaba, September 1, 2017).

At this point, I cannot resist some specific writing advice: A major (but easy-to-fix) problem I see with writing this relatively easy methods chapter is that students are taught, or learn by reading models from the academic literature, to describe their procedures and findings using passive voice—"X was done"—rather than "I did X." Many established academics and novice scholars and dissertation writers follow this convention, believing, I guess, that it lends "objectivity" to their reporting, as Sword (2009) reported from a survey she did of academic journal articles in the social sciences. Countering this view, she said that "the days are long past when scientists and social scientists were absolutely forbidden to use the word 'I' in their academic publications" (p. 329). Nevertheless, few authors in her sample used first person. Sword continued: "Apparently the old myth that Impersonal = Objective = Scientifically Superior still holds firm in many social scientists' minds" (p. 330).

I think I am not alone in preferring academic writing that states clearly who is doing what. However, using active voice does not mean that you have to begin every sentence with *I*. There are ways to balance first person pronouns as active agents and subjects of sentences with other nouns. I wrote about this in

Before the Dissertation, and since then am increasingly convinced that the power and clarity of academic writing only improves with active agents and actions. The writing experts have concluded this, too. The passive voice only obscures who did what in your study. Even the notoriously conservative APA (American Psychological Association) tells writers to use active voice and to tell clearly what they did: "Verbs are vigorous, direct communicators. Use the active rather than the passive voice, and select tense or mood carefully" (*APA Manual,* 2010, p. 77; *APA Manual,* 2020, section 4.13). Passive voice is preferred only when the agent of an action is unknown or not important for clarity. Other well-known proponents of good writing have for many years advocated the use of first person and active voice to make writing clear and strong (Lanham, 2007; Sword, 2012; Williams & Colomb, 2012; Zinsser, 2006, 2012), in spite of lingering timidity that social scientists have about using *I* (Quinlan, 2013).

Writing the Conceptual Framework and Literature Review

A fundamental background section that can frame and inform the whole dissertation is a review of theories, concepts, and empirical studies, presented together or in separate chapters. Such a review tells readers what assumptions and framing theories ground your study, and what empirical research has already been done on topics related to yours. By writing these chapters, you show how your dissertation will fit into a philosophical tradition, a field, and a body of empirical work. You have done your conceptual and empirical readings (see *Before the Dissertation*, Chapter 6) and made your notes and comments, so it seems as though writing the literature review should be easy. Just summarize and comment on a lot of readings, perhaps separating them into conceptual and empirical works.

Well, sort of. One result of this simplified version of a literature review is that novice writers tend to comment on their readings one by one, without considering a vision of the whole. Each reading is written about separately, often with author names fronted rather than topics, and then presented in some kind of order (alphabetical, thematic, chronological...). The summaries are straightforward, and the comments are not cross-referenced or synthesized. However, a literature review that provides a background for the whole project is not the same as an annotated bibliography, which is what this kind of separate summary writing looks like. An annotated bibliography is easy to write. A literature review is not. Whether the main criterion is thoroughness or relevance (see the debate between Boote & Beile, 2005, and Maxwell, 2006), a good literature review synthesizes ideas from readings into a kind of narrative or argument—a research story (Feak & Swales, 2009)—that contributes to the whole.

Writing about What You Found

Writing about what you found in your dissertation research is fairly straightforward, although complications can arise when your findings are based on lengthy conversational interviews and descriptive observations. Such findings are quite difficult to select from the huge amount of data and then to present in an organized cohesive manner. In all cases, dissertation writers, like all researchers, need to find the patterns and themes in their data, and then put them together in a way that eventually results in a vision of the whole, one that represents a particular version of "truth" constructed by the writer. Findings can easily look piecemeal, particularly if presented in various separate forms (narratives, descriptions, tables and figures, direct quotes). Constructing a vision of the whole from the pieces, or into which the pieces can fit as you would a jigsaw puzzle, turns out to be both a challenging and creative task. This is why it is helpful to craft (and periodically re-craft) a vision of the whole—a canvas rather than a jigsaw puzzle—throughout the dissertation writing process.

Discussing and Concluding Your Dissertation

The vision of the whole is particularly pertinent in Discussion sections, where the findings come together in a more holistic vision of what you as researcher have found to be meaningful in your data and how your findings connect to other work that has been done in your topic area, reviewed by you earlier. In other words, the trick is not just to write about the synthesized meanings in your data, but also to connect meanings back to your readings and to show how your dissertation project moves our knowledge forward in some way. I think I am not unique in finding this section a difficult one to write, particularly while maintaining a vision of the whole. If you feel overwhelmed, give yourself time; get help; go back to your purpose statements; review your most relevant readings; think about the readings and connect your findings to them; consult your adviser; talk to liked-minded friends and colleagues; and think. Walk and think; shower and think; doze and think; sit quietly and think.

Introducing Your Dissertation

I conclude this chapter with a brief comment on the Introduction to a dissertation. Once everything else is done, you can then draft, or finish drafting and revising, your Introduction. Please don't try to finish this as a first step, even if you start it this way. It is really a last step. It is at this point, at the end, when you can see, feel, and embody the vision of the whole, because you have sweat blood and tears to document all the parts of this vision in the canvas that is your dissertation. The Introduction and the

Abstract are now ready to be finished. You are now ready to tell readers in a succinct few pages what the study is about, why and how you did it, why it is important, and what it means.

SUMMARY OF MAIN POINTS

1. A vision of the whole dissertation can help guide all the work that follows.
2. Titles, readings, and early drafts of sections can help writers craft a vision of the whole dissertation.
3. Introductions are probably best written and revised last, after the dissertation draft has been completed and it is clear what the dissertation is about and how it was done.

SUGGESTIONS FOR DISCUSSION AND REFLECTION

1. In your experience and that of classmates and colleagues, how important do you think it is to develop a vision of the whole dissertation at early stages of the process, such as at the proposal stage? How do you go about constructing this vision?
2. If you have completed your data collection and started writing drafts of different sections of your dissertation, do you have a vision of what the whole dissertation will look like? How has this vision changed from the proposal stage?
3. In your particular case, how might a vision of the whole dissertation help you with the actual writing of each of the chapters and sections? If you find this approach not to be helpful, why not? What other approach(es) have you used or could you use?

4. Have you experimented with different titles and subtitles for your dissertation? If so, how have these helped you maintain a vision for what you need to do? If not, do you think it would be a useful exercise? Why or why not?
5. What choices have you made up to now about what chapters and sections of the dissertation you will work on first, second, next? What is the reasoning behind your choices?

Chapter 3

Relations with Supervisors and Advisers

"[S]upervisors themselves are not always well equipped to develop the writing skills of their supervisees. ... "[Yet] the supervisor/student relationship is critical to successful doctoral studies."

—Cally Guerin et al., 2017, pp. A-96 and A-97

"[D]irect instruction about writing is not easy for many supervisors, who frequently struggle to explain the very discursive practices that they themselves have mastered."

—Anthony Paré, 2017, p. 413

This chapter deals with the sensitive topic of dissertation writers' relationships with supervisors (a term I will use interchangeably with *advisers*) and other influential faculty during the writing stage of dissertation work, a topic covered partially in *Before the Dissertation* (Chapter 7). This relationship typically takes place in person, but long distance relationships via electronic media are also common these days, especially at the dissertation writing stage. In whatever form it takes, the relationship works best when interactions happen regularly, assuming compatibility between supervisor and student. These relationships also work best if the project supervisor is well versed and interested in students' topics and preferred methods, is experienced at recognizing early warning signs of problems (Manathunga, 2005), understands something about students' cultures and languages (Manathunga, 2014), and is around long enough to see the project through to its end. Ideally, the relationship involves mentoring, not just dissertation advising, but this is not always the case. In either case, a smooth or a troubled relationship between supervisors and students can affect not only students' writing, but also the eventual success or failure of a dissertation project or even whether students complete the doctoral program (Zhao, Golde, & McCormick, 2007).

Relationships, both in person and online, can be characterized in the extreme either by neglect or by excessive control and hand-holding at the writing stage, both of which will create tensions between supervisors and students. Likewise, students and supervisors may have compatible or incompatible personalities, styles, interests, knowledge, and goals. The challenges can be daunting. Both students and supervisors need to understand each others' mutual expectations, deal with possible conflicts, and know how to manage the relationship so that students get what they need from supervisors without feeling intimidated by them, and so that supervisors do not burn out from overwork when actual writing is taking place.

I recall from my own doctoral dissertation days how a few trusted classmates would often talk about (well, gossip about) their advisers and their relationships with them during both research assistantships and dissertation writing. Our experiences differed, even when we were working with the same person. I note here that I will not write about affairs or scandals or crushes or serious neuroses, but I learned over time and more recently from internet searches that these happened then and probably happen now. In this chapter, however, I am concerned with influences of the academic aspects of the supervisory relationship on dissertation writing. This chapter is an especially difficult one to write just because there are so many diverse experiences that could be described (Sternberg, 1981). The range is immense between neglect and excessive control as is the range between emotional and intellectual aspects of the supervisor-advisee relationship. Readers will need to add their own stories to the collection.

In my case, during dissertation writing, my contacts with my main adviser, secondary adviser, and minor adviser were fairly infrequent, and happened only when I had some piece of writing to share with them. They did not contact me otherwise, and I did not often consult with them unless we had a draft of something to talk about. In those days, especially when I was still living near campus, I turned in paper copies of my word-processed chapter drafts, and my main adviser provided handwritten feedback on them, in styles that ranged from rather lengthy comments and questions, to a word or two or possibly only a check mark from other committee members. In some cases, a faculty member would revise or rewrite small portions of text, usually just a few sentences, much easier to do these days by computer.

I had no idea then what the norm was (if any) for adviser-student interactions. Each of the three main people I worked with had different areas of expertise, so I tended to expect some commentary on the entire project only from my primary adviser. However, she did not know much about second language issues, so had no way to evaluate parts of my dissertation work that dealt with participants who were not L1 speakers of English. She commented at one point that she was learning about such issues from me, indicating that the relationship was mutually beneficial. I don't know how common such a reciprocal relationship is between supervisor and student, but it certainly seems like a good idea, especially when a student has more specialized knowledge about a topic than a faculty member does. The other two faculty I worked with commented on aspects or particular chapters that suited their knowledge and interests, and only a few times during the entire dissertation writing process. I was lucky to have pretty good chemistry with these people, and not to suffer from some of the personality conflicts that some other students had with their advisers.

Compatibility, Conflict, and Expectations

It is difficult to comprehend how profoundly the compatibility or conflict between supervisors and doctoral students can affect their relationship until one has experienced a relationship that goes well and one that goes badly. When I began supervising my own doctoral students, I reflected on my relationships with my own advisers and also began reading some of the literature on doctoral supervising (see some discussion of this work in this chapter). Through discussions and consultations, I also learned something about my students' and their classmates' relationships with key faculty and with other advisers, and of course got a sense of how the students that I was advising felt about me. It was not all easy going. Some students who did not feel encouraged enough by people they were working with changed advisers if they could (I picked up a few students this way and also lost a couple), or dropped out of the program. Others suffered under incompatible goals and styles with advisers and were torn about suggestions they disagreed with or found difficult to follow. I observed that it was often difficult for students to negotiate with advisers, given power differences. A long time ago, Sternberg (1981) described some of the supervising styles that can create problems for students, such as "The Young Turk Professor," "The

Sadistic Professor,""The Passive-Aggressive Professor,""The Sexist Professor," and "The Jealous or Envious Professor" (pp. 148–151). Working with a perfectionist adviser seems to be especially difficult, or with one who expects writing to show "mastery and control" as an outcome rather than as an unreachable goal in the process of learning (Barnacle & Dall'Alba, 2014). Uncertainty is a normal state of affairs in intellectual inquiry throughout a career, and sensitive advisers can usefully help doctoral students come to terms with this inevitability and to recognize it as a positive and motivating phenomenon.

Personality or style conflicts between adviser and student during dissertation writing are a serious matter, not easily resolved. My one serious problem with a student came early in my doctoral supervising career and involved an event that surprised me greatly and for which I was totally unprepared. With students working within a cohort system, I tended to encourage them to share work, readings, and issues with each other one-on-one or in study groups, for the purpose of mutual support, and so sometimes asked them to discuss something with classmates who were working on similar problems. The student in question accused me of revealing secrets about his topic to another student, fearing that another student might steal his ideas. This same student also accused me of prejudice against him for giving him a grade slightly lower than he expected (A- instead of A). I was quite flabbergasted in both instances and not sure what to do, beyond talking to the student and defending my choices. But I felt intimidated by this student, as he probably did by me, and he did not continue working with me. In fact, he left the program before finishing his doctorate. Since then, I have tried to assess how compatible a student and I are before we get too deeply into a dissertation advising relationship, and to be able to justify comments and suggestions to each student if needed. Comments and suggestions during supervisory work are a normal two-way occurrence, and if either supervisor or student feels attacked, disrespected, not listened to, or misunderstood, the relationship and the work will suffer.

I have also tried to give each new doctoral dissertation writer I work with a clear idea of my expectations before we begin a semester of work together, and to learn from them what their expectations are. This information initially takes the form of a general memo to all my current students, and then evolves into individual consultations as needed. Whether I am working long-distance or in person with someone, I hope for regular contact with the student, not just when the student has a piece of writing to give me. Waiting for a chapter draft to be submitted before students and I consult can lead to many weeks with no contact until the end of the term, when it is too late for me to provide ongoing guidance. I have found it difficult at times to convince students how important regular contact is during dissertation work, particularly if they have had a different experience with other faculty members during course work or faculty from previous degree work who expect nothing from a student until the end of a term. What a wasted opportunity for mentoring and for learning! As a dissertation adviser, I hope to think along with students and to participate regularly in their development over several years, but without hand-holding or controlling what they do. Moreover, I do my best to convince students that I do not know everything. For example, they cannot expect me to give them a full reading list about their topics or to know in detail how to analyze data using techniques I am not familiar with. In other words, the dissertation writers I work with necessarily have much to learn on their own or from other faculty, and therefore have much to teach me. We need regular contact to be able to learn from each other. In all cases, by the time they are finished with their dissertation writing, the students are the experts on their topics and methods, not I. It may sound selfish to say, but if I am not learning anything in my relationship with a dissertation writer, I find the experience unfulfilling.

How Do Supervisors Understand Their Roles at the Doctoral Dissertation Writing Stage?

Much of the literature on doctoral supervision comes from European and British-system contexts (such as Australia, the U.K., New Zealand) in which doctoral work consists primarily of students doing research and writing a thesis-dissertation, rather than their engaging in several years of course work before beginning the dissertation research, as is the case in many U.S. universities. But whether the context is outside or within the United States, the relationship between a supervisor and a student who is at the dissertation-writing stage can affect the quality and success of the dissertation-writing experience (Guerin et al., 2017, p. A-97).

Literature on doctoral supervising from studies around the world supports this conclusion about the importance of the relationship and the need for new supervisors to learn to avoid or deal with problems that might arise, such as student defensiveness that gets in the way of learning (Feather & McDermott, 2014). Feather and McDermott noted that new doctoral supervisors might learn about program administration, but not about "the realities of supervision; that is, the emotions, the mentoring of students (both domestic and international), and the softer issues of dealing with students and their needs" (p. 169). Such studies point out that "both the quality and the quantity of doctoral supervision have been identified as central determinants of the doctoral journey" (Cornér, Löfström, & Pyhältö, 2017, p. 91), including students' experiences of stress, burnout, and failure to complete their projects when the relationship does not go well. Given that writing is the main activity in the production of a dissertation, "the writing opportunities that students experience are powerfully shaped by the relationship between student and supervisor" (Cotterall, 2011, p. 414). However, it is likely that not many dissertation supervisors understand or conceptualize their roles as writing teachers or as contributors to students' emotional well-being. Instead they often see themselves as managers and gatekeepers, not negotiators, and students may see them the same way (Jazvac-Martek, Chen, & McAlpine, 2011). One result of this attitude by supervisors is that dissertation writers can feel isolated and neglected, while at the same time believing that the isolation and neglect are normal. After all, isn't one of the goals of doctoral work to produce "independent scholars"?

Supervisors' Influences on Dissertation Writers' Emotional States

Regardless of how supervisors envision their roles in relation to your actual dissertation writing, the reality seems to be that the supervisor-student relationship can be a deeply emotional and stressful one (Burford, 2017; Cotterall, 2013; Li & Seale, 2007; Sternberg, 1981; Strandler, Johansson, Wisker, & Claesson, 2014; Wisker & Robinson, 2016). Students need to determine how much agency they have in that relationship, as well as attend to relationships in their lives beyond that with a supervisor (Hopwood, 2010). Emotions can run high. The only way for supervisors to avoid the emotional aspect of the relationship is for them simply not to be involved with your writing at all. If on the other hand they feel even partially responsible for your emotional well-being, in addition to your eventual success at dissertation writing and your evolving scholarly identities (Botelho de Magalhães, Cotterall, & Mideros, 2019; Cotterall, 2015), the work of supervising can be as deeply gratifying as it is stressful. Supervisors, after all, are helping doctoral dissertation writers become certain kinds of people—helping you develop identities as scholars—and helping you to succeed in this endeavor through guidance in dissertation writing.

At the same time, to be most effective in their supervising activities, faculty need to have their own levels of stress under control, such as stresses that result from pressures at work, their own obligations to write and publish, and their personal, sometimes conflicted and emotional, responses to working with individual graduate students. In general, pressures on faculty have increased as universities have taken on some of the relentless (and I think misapplied) expectations for productivity from the business world (Wisker & Robinson, 2016), in which faculty success is measured by metrics such as publication records and how many PhD students they have seen through to completion. But for the purposes of this chapter, I am interested in the connections and responsibilities that faculty feel toward their students who are writing dissertations or publishable papers that they need to complete in order to graduate. The connections are both emotional and intellectual and so potentially sources of stress for faculty as well as for students.

For those supervisors who closely monitor their students' dissertation work, such stress can result not only from the labor-intensive nature of their help with your writing, but also from ongoing decisions they need to make about how involved to become (if at all) in your emotional lives. (I will not write about supervisor-student affairs and seductions, but they are probably more common than we would like to believe. Avoid them, please.) Many questions hover. Is it the job of dissertation supervisors to help you avoid becoming discouraged? To convince your to persist in your efforts at writing? To help you build and maintain your confidence? To dissipate your fears? To ensure trust between you and them? No doubt some supervisors will respond that such efforts are not part of their responsibilities in helping students with their dissertation writing and that emotional ties of any kind with students are either unnecessary or off-limits.

On the other hand, to what extent are you as doctoral students responsible for identifying problems in your relationships with supervisors and for being proactive in addressing the problems? What is the line between the need for you to develop autonomy and to learn to forge a socially constructed intellectual life, including in the process of creating single-authored documents like doctoral dissertations or papers for publication? Are supervisors expected to help you write and revise such work to the point where it can be seen as a co-constructed knowledge product, one in which the supervisor is emotionally invested along with the student? And a fundamental question asks how much supervisors actually know about writing in L1 and L2, from their experience, from knowledge of the writing literature, or from courses in supervisor development (Guerin et al., 2017).

In my own experience as a doctoral student, I witnessed numerous cases of fraught emotional relationships between advisers and students. I can write about these only generally in the interest of preserving confidentiality, but can say the following, which I am guessing will be recognized by any doctoral student who has spent several years in a program. First, personality and style conflicts between some faculty and students are inevitable. Usually by the dissertation writing stage, students know whom they will be able to work with smoothly and whom they should avoid. Difficulties arise when students cannot choose whom to work with, and so face months or even years of emotional tension with a faculty member they might not be compatible with. Tensions may be great, such as in the case of major personality conflicts, or less severe, such as in the case of differing expectations with regard to an adviser's responses to students' drafts. For instance, I had a strong emotional response to a faculty member who rewrote some passages in my writing rather than suggesting what I might do myself. My ownership of the text felt impinged upon and my feelings of resistance and mistrust probably prevented me from learning what I could from this person. In another case, my defenses went up when a professor suggested that if I were to work with him, I would need to adhere to his guidance unquestioningly, and thus give up research methods and writing styles that I was particularly attracted to. This emotional response of resistance to having some aspect of my work taken over by someone else was one of the strongest I felt during my doctoral work. The negative side of this emotional response during dissertation writing could be that I resisted changes and suggestions that might have improved my dissertation—I was a novice scholar after all. I do not know where or how to draw the line between the drive for dissertation writers to own their work and to learn from and depend on others, but can say that figuring out how to balance and negotiate such expectations is potentially an emotional tug of war.

In sum, in the midst of doctoral dissertation writing, it is difficult for students to understand with clarity and comprehension what their relationship should be with a main adviser and with various other faculty that might be helping, particularly given that each relationship no doubt differs greatly depending on individual and departmental expectations (see some of Sternberg's, 1981, earlier comments on this relationship). Among other difficulties, supervisors can be skilled at research but not know how to deal with problems with students (Wisker & Robinson, 2016, p. 4). It is difficult to prescribe, for example, what a supervisor's role should be in helping students build confidence in themselves and in their developing scholarship, in helping them improve their writing, in allaying their discouragement and fear, and in promoting students' willingness to persist and trust in themselves and in their supervisor's guidance. Clearly the two extremes of excessive neglect and excessive control and involvement are best avoided. On the other hand, mutual understanding of the stresses involved in both dissertation writing and in supervising will benefit supervisors and dissertation writers alike.

What Do/Should Doctoral Students Notice about Their Supervisor's/Adviser's Stress Level?

Doctoral students might be too absorbed in their own stresses about dissertation writing to notice much that is going on around them. After all, a certain single-mindedness is needed to get to the end of your project. During actual dissertation writing, you might meet infrequently with your advisers, such as only when you have a complete chapter draft to share. When you do meet with your advisers, it is likely that you will expect all attention to focus on you and the drafts you have written, and not on your adviser's state of well-being.

If true, it is odd that doctoral students might not think much about their advisers' health and well-being, given the role that advisers play in your successes and failures and in your overall experiences in graduate school. An ill or overly stressed adviser cannot provide you with effective guidance. The importance of the supervisor in the dissertation process was documented in a study of 20 male and female doctoral students at an American university. The researchers found that "Almost all participants considered their supervisors as one of the most important factors shaping their experiences as doctoral students" (Kurtz-Costes, Andrews Helmke, Ülkü-Steiner, 2006, p. 143). This perspective, like others, such as those discussed by Halse and Malfroy (2010; Halse, 2011) and Russell-Pinson and Harris (2019), acknowledges that supervisors and advisers play an enormous role in doctoral students' experiences, including how students experience and manage stress. However, the issue of supervisor or adviser stress is less often studied, even though the stresses that advisers experience will affect the quality of advising they can provide their students. Whether or not supervisors acknowledge this influence of stress on the quality of their advising, it is there, and all participants know it.

On the one hand, a response to this issue could be: It's none of students' business to be concerned about their adviser's health or levels of stress. Although it could be helpful for advisers to know something about what stresses you are experiencing while writing your dissertation (opinions may differ here), why would you need to know anything about stresses in the lives of your advisers or any other faculty member unless the person is truly incapacitated? Such knowledge could alter the power balance in favor of students, reducing a faculty member's aura of authority, making the faculty member feel vulnerable, and reducing trust between students and faculty during crucial periods of dissertation writing. After all, many of you in doctoral programs, especially in teacher education programs, are similar in age to or older than some faculty and are often experienced teachers and members of professional communities. You could thus potentially intimidate a faculty member who is a novice at supervising and who might be experiencing his or her own problems, including the relentless scramble for promotion and tenure. Nevertheless, it is important that you see your supervisors as people whom you can trust to provide good guidance on both the process and content of a dissertation. Supervisors, for their part, need to manage their health and stress levels in order to provide competent guidance. In this respect, a supervisor's health and well-being are indeed the business of a dissertation writer.

Mutual Trust, Respect, and Communication

Students also need to see their supervisors as authority figures who have the power to help them succeed or, if things don't work out, who might contribute to their failure. Trust and good communication and negotiating skills are thus essential, in particular between students and supervisors who do not share first languages or cultures. If you do not share languages or cultures, you might not fully understand what individual supervisors expect communication to be like during dissertation writing, including how proactive you should be in requesting help with your writing. For cultural or linguistic reasons, some of you might be reluctant to speak up in meetings with supervisors who expect active participation, with the result that you end up not getting the help you need (Cargill, 2000). As Cargill concluded in her study of two pairs of international students and their supervisors in Australia, some international students, and perhaps L1 English users as well, need very clear signals about when and how they should speak up during in-person meetings, and I presume in online communication as well. Trust needs to build over time, with supervisors attending as best they can to signs that trust needs attending to and that mutual expectations are well understood. Otherwise, balanced negotiating cannot take place.

For such trust to develop, both you and supervisors need to recognize that supervising styles are likely to differ not only according to cultures and languages of supervisor and student but also according to individual personalities and contextual issues. For example, a supervisor who is experiencing stress for whatever reasons (overwork, burnout, pressures to publish, conflicts with students or other faculty, problems at home) will possibly have trouble relating to and negotiating with doctoral students in a consistently patient and helpful manner. Effective supervision, unsurprisingly, is linked to supervisor well-being (Wisker & Robinson, 2016), a topic that has not been studied much, perhaps because it is quite sensitive and personal. I recall a case of a young professor newly hired at a prestigious school who easily lost his patience with some students, snapped at them, and made them feel inadequate, in spite of tranquilizers he was taking. Another professor was trying to advise doctoral students while she herself was undertaking a job search, having lost in her efforts to secure a tenured job at the university. Another professor was dealing with her own health problems and those of a daughter, while simultaneously trying to care for her professor husband, who had just had a stroke. Yet others were known to have alcohol problems and some consequences of these problems related to mood, memory, and efficiency of their work with students. The examples I give are not for the most part those of novice professors, but of well-established and in some cases well-known people.

Such problems are probably more than you need or want to know about your supervisors, but they affect the kinds and quality of guidance that you get. They are also problems that are normal in the lives of professional people and students. How much of their own lives, then, do supervisors try to hide from students and colleagues? How much do students hide from supervisors? How do doctoral students and their advisers decide how much they need to know about each other in order for effective guidance to take place? It is not clear how much mutual knowledge and understanding is needed for a successful supervisor-student relationship, particularly at the dissertation writing stage. Perhaps the details are not needed, but certainly all participants will benefit from acknowledging the complexities and secrets of real life that lurk in the background. These complexities potentially influence the supervising relationship, and the quality of this relationship will inevitably influence the dissertation writing.

Perhaps a bottom line in the supervising relationship is that you need to feel confident, not fearful, in approaching and engaging with your dissertation supervisor for questions and consultations, and even for consolation, if things are not going well. You need to know that help is available and that negotiation is possible when there are disagreements. You need to know that it is possible to change advisers if serious problems cannot be resolved. On the other hand, when the relationship and the writing are going well, both supervisors and you can turn off your computers at the end of the day, knowing that your jobs have been well done and that you are both on a journey that involves mutual learning and respect.

SUMMARY OF MAIN POINTS

1. The supervisor-dissertation writer relationship can determine in part how successful the dissertation writing is in terms of quality of the dissertation and timing of its completion.
2. Supervisors are rarely fully expert in students' choices of dissertation topics or methodologies and methods.
3. Dissertation writers need to learn and negotiate what supervisors expect during the actual writing of the dissertation. Expectations are likely to differ according to cultural setting, department or discipline, and personalities.
4. Dissertation writing can be an emotional experience, as can dissertation supervising. Emotions and well-being of both students and supervisors need to be monitored carefully.
5. Real life issues influence the student-supervisor relationship, even if details remain unacknowledged.

SUGGESTIONS FOR DISCUSSION AND REFLECTION

1. Are you primarily a solitary or a collegial writer? How does your preference, if any, for solitude or collegiality change according to the particular dissertation writing task you are working on?
2. How much choice do you have in selecting an adviser for your dissertation writing? If you have a choice, what do you look for in an ideal adviser at the writing stage? Do you feel you could change advisers in the midst of dissertation writing if the relationship is not going well?

3. At this point in your dissertation writing, how much help, and what kinds of help, are you getting from your supervisor-adviser and from other faculty? Are you satisfied with this help? If not, how might you improve the situation?
4. What stresses, if any, are you experiencing in your relationships with your supervisor-adviser or other key faculty who are helping you with dissertation writing? How do you explain the stresses, and what ideas do you have for alleviating them so that your writing might continue smoothly?

Chapter 4

Perfectionism and Other Maladies

"Over the past year, I've worked with more than 400 dissertation writers, and I've seen over and over again that isolation, perfectionism, and procrastination are the three biggest threats to completion."

—Kerry Ann Rockquemore, 2016

This chapter covers affective obstacles to efficient and steady writing such as perfectionism and the maladies that blossom in its wake. These maladies include guilt that accompanies the "should" disease; self-sabotaging behaviors such as writer's block; misguided expectations, or just feeling overwhelmed; a desire for or belief in the impossible goal of mastery and control; and procrastination resulting from fear of failure (covered further in Chapter 8). I do not speculate deeply about the causes of perfectionism, blocks, and procrastination, but instead explore the compulsion that some dissertation writers have to try to perfect their high-stakes work before they submit it for evaluation, even when we cannot easily define "perfection" in a dissertation. The compulsion feeds writers' tendencies to leave work undone and to be distracted by other important activities (see Chapter 8). A parallel drive for perfection and its associated maladies might also characterize the attitudes and behaviors of some supervisors, whose excessively high standards for their students' dissertation work could be counterproductive. Students can easily come to believe that their work will never satisfy their supervisors. In other words, the negative consequences of perfectionism, including self-handicapping (Kearns, Forbes, Gardiner, & Marshall, 2008), whether practiced by students or their supervisors, can actually prevent dissertation writers from completing their projects, which in the writers' eyes, and maybe even in their supervisors' eyes, may never seem "good enough."

This chapter does not offer tricks to cure perfectionism, but aims to help you understand perfectionist tendencies and to help your supervisors understand what you, and even they, might be experiencing. A thematic thread running through the chapter asks "how good is good enough?" This question is not about perfection, but is a practical one about completing a doctoral project that is good enough to satisfy advisers, other faculty, the university, and of course doctoral candidates themselves. If you are not a perfectionist, and if you are confident in what you are doing, do not have impossibly high standards, and have evidence of your successes, you are one of the fortunate few, and have my whole-hearted approval to skip this chapter.

Perfectionism Is the Enemy of Completion

It is not surprising that some dissertation writers are compelled to perfect their high-stakes work before they submit it for evaluation, even when we cannot easily define "perfection" in a dissertation. You want to get it right, and to receive praise and acceptance, as well as a passing grade on the document you submit, and may even unrealistically strive for "perfection," as in the case of some L2 writers who aim for native-like English (Mochizuki, 2019). Yet we know that perfectionism is the enemy of completion. If the dissertation draft or drafts of dissertation papers for publication never seem good enough or never complete enough, you will hesitate to submit them to your supervisors or other faculty for feedback—one of the many reasons that dissertation writers procrastinate and develop self-handicapping behaviors (Kearns, Gardiner, & Marshall, 2008; see Chapter 8). The problem worsens if you are simultaneously working full time or at several part time jobs, or if you have overcommitted to participating in the enormous range of possible academic activities open to or required of you in your doctoral programs. If you have not developed skills of time management, the ability to say "no," and a realistic goal of passing rather than perfection, you may never complete your project, which in your eyes always needs more work before being shared with evaluators.

Some dissertation writers who pursue perfection may also suffer from what I call the "should disease," in which they feel compelled to follow prescriptions, templates, how-to guides, and advice by supervisors and other experts (discussed further below in the section on Self-Sabotaging Behaviors). Some of this advice, much of it very useful, has been around for a long time (see Becker, 1986; Sternberg, 1981), and more recent advice these days can be found on websites with a few key search words ("tips for doctoral dissertation writers" for example). Many of the resources offer writers strategies and steps for completing their writing by deadlines. Such resources might tell you what you should do, how you should do the tasks associated with writing, when you should do them, and in what order. Both supervisors and how-to guidebooks and websites certainly try to offer helpful prescriptions for getting the dissertation writing done. They discuss time management, daily writing strategies such as setting word minimums and time-on-task goals, deciding the order of writing (what should be done first, second, third…), and strategies for sharing writing and doing revisions. If you are a perfectionist dissertation writer, you will likely strive to follow all this advice and more, but possibly to the detriment of your progress.

Literature review writing offers a good example of how perfectionism can impede progress. In one engaging book, supervisors are cautioned that one of their roles is to help students understand that writing a literature review is not just about summarizing readings, but is more like "persuading an octopus into a jar" (Kamler & Thomson, 2014, Chapter 3; see other wonderful images and metaphors that workshop students came up with, pp. 35-36). The goal is to show by the end of the review why the study is needed. As useful as these suggestions and those in other guidebooks are, they don't guarantee perfection or even completion. Moreover, you and even your supervisors can be overcome by guilt and a sense of incompetence if you can't live up to the guidelines, steps, or models you have chosen to follow. Perfectionism that stems from trying to follow externally imposed advice can thus lead to paralysis. In all cases, you need to identify your own obstacles to and strategies for getting your writing done, which may or may not accord with advice in guide books, on websites, or offered by supervisors. Whatever strategies you follow, you will certainly need to recognize that the goal of perfection is a dead-end street for most of us.

Some dissertation writers and supervisors who chase after perfection may not be able to resist this pursuit, having been born and raised with perfectionist tendencies from childhood. Whether such tendencies are genetic or inculcated may not matter as much as the fact that they have been dogging these well-meaning academics most of their lives. One colleague, well along in his successful career, is tempted to blame his mother, or at least his childhood desires to please her. He wrote of her:

> She was intense—a hyper critical force of nature—she wanted things right, so I grew up alternatively either knowing I couldn't make her very happy (which actually I think was character-building in a way) or trying to make

> her happy. She was a loving mother—I never felt unloved—but very difficult to make happy, especially for a slow developer/typical little boy who didn't know which way was up or down. (email, anonymous colleague, December 12, 2018)

With such a beginning, this colleague believes he has been a perfectionist all his life, a characteristic that he found continually interfered in the past with his mentoring of graduate students and with his ability to complete his own writing projects, including his dissertation and book projects that followed in particular. He indicated that the interference stemmed in part from his unrealistically high expectations. The positive side to such tendencies is significant, however, particularly in the academic world. This colleague wrote: "It's been good in the sense that I found a profession and field where I could be a perfectionist, and it yielded certain benefits, including being an exacting reader and writer." Not bad qualities for both dissertation supervisors and writers! For the shorter writings, he has found that his perfectionism "operates productively (just writing draft after draft, basically, until I 'get it right')." The dilemma for the perfectionist dissertation writer or supervisor, of course, is that you might not have time to write draft after draft and supervisors might not have time or patience to read and comment and to provide you with endless feedback until the draft meets their standards. There comes a time, all too quickly, when both you and supervisors just have to stop (see Chapter 10).

I find such stories fascinating, because in some ways I am blessed by not being a compulsive perfectionist except for my attention to grammar and spelling, but sometimes wish I were more of one. My own work usually eventually gets done without being perfected (whatever that means), although I have on occasion given up on a writing project. I am not proud of this, and always urge students not to give up if they have strong reasons for continuing and can set aside any illusions of perfection they might be harboring. Dissertations that I help doctoral students write manage to get finished without being Pulitzer Prize material. It helps that there are no letter or numerical grades on these dissertations. They pass, or they don't. The "perfect" dissertation sits on the library shelf or in the electronic library, usually unread by more than a handful of people, alongside the less-than-perfect ones. The perfectionist, however, no doubt feels a special pride at completing such a major project in a way that results in a beautiful—not just competent—product, and possibly one that leads to one or more publications later.

Although I am not a true perfectionist, my standards are high for myself and for dissertation writers. Content must be rich and interesting and not just repeat what has been said before. The writing must be engaging and coherent if not of literary quality. I also have (as my mother did) a genetic predisposition toward admiring "correct" grammar, a notion that is disputed these days by the lingua franca and World Englishes people, who have mostly been concerned, to be sure, with oral language (Galloway & Rose, 2015; Holliday, 2009; Jenkins, 2014; Kachru, 1997; Kachru, Kachru, & Nelson, 2006; Seidlhofer, 2011; but see Hartse & Kubota, 2014). They all, however, resist the notion that one dominant standard of English must prevail in the (academic) world. Change is slow.

But even without adhering to a single dominant model of academic writing, academic writers like me still believe in some kind of standard, and certainly in consistency, clarity, and concision in high stakes writing like a dissertation or other doctoral assessments (Pinker, 2014; Sword, 2012; Williams, 1997; Williams & Bizup, 2015). I value and take pleasure in editing and proofreading my own and others' work and I love beautiful language. Nevertheless, my concerns with proofing and polishing provide me some insights into the malady of perfectionism, and into perfectionists' fears that their names will be associated with work (their own or their students') that is less than perfect. I confess that I notice in published work as well as in completed dissertations (my own included) the presence of typos, misspelled names, lists that are not grammatically parallel, nonstandard punctuation, verbs that don't agree with their subjects, as well as generally inelegant writing. I notice when one sentence or one paragraph doesn't flow smoothly into the next and I notice inconsistencies in referencing styles or reference lists that diverge in tiny ways from accepted conventions. (I once noticed a comma in one of my own reference lists that was mistakenly italicized.) These are small problems that can easily be fixed in the finished work, but the perfectionist has trouble moving on if they are not fixed now. It continues to be difficult for me to separate the content of writing from the way it is presented, even in my drafts. (I realize that such confessions do come across sounding like those of a closet perfectionist....)

Drafts are supposed to be different. My tendencies toward mild perfectionism in what I expect from myself and doctoral students in writing, even at the draft stage, counter some of the most hallowed and long-standing advice in the fields of both first and second language writing. Save your correcting and perfecting till the end, as Flower and Hayes (1981) in first language composition and Zamel (1983) in ESL composition told us long ago, and use the drafting process the way experts do, to discover meaning (Zamel, 1982, 1983) and to get the basic ideas turned into words. Write "with power," without being constrained excessively by academic conventions, and if you feel blocked, ignore your audience (Elbow, 1981, 1994, 1995). Do this writing and thinking without worrying about perfecting a draft that will only be changed and polished later. Expert writers, it is said, do their correcting at the end of the writing process, at the revising and proofing stages, not as they are generating ideas and text.

I have studied this advice, and to some extent believe it. It makes good sense. However, this observation is not actually true of all expert writers, the most extreme example of which I have found is Annie Dillard. Dillard has claimed to need to perfect each sentence before moving on to the next (Dillard, 1989). A good writing day for someone like Dillard might result in one paragraph. I am not about to tell Annie Dillard that she must change her ways. Her writing, spare as it is, is elegant, but it might take someone like her a decade to finish a doctoral dissertation (she survived just fine with a master's degree).

Though I am not a perfectionist in the style of Dillard, my genetic predisposition leads me to pick away at small things in every draft, from first to last, and to be irritated (unfairly) with doctoral dissertation writers who give me what feels like "sloppy" work. I want dissertation writers to proofread even their first drafts to me, and to cite and reference their literature meticulously from the earliest stages of their dissertation writing, most importantly for accurate record keeping but also for aesthetic reasons. The best I have been able to do to control this tendency is to explain to students that perfectionism can be counter-productive, to apologize when necessary when they see me tending in this direction, and to assure them that it is indeed the final draft of their dissertations that will require the most meticulous revising and proofreading. Dissertations of course require that writers craft and polish much larger issues in their writing, not just the mechanics of language—accuracy and depth of content, logic of an argument, coherence and flow of the whole. However, a true perfectionist, whether student or supervisor, will have so many layers, embeddings, and dimensions of writing at the larger and smaller levels to worry about that he or she may never be able to finish a writing project.

As a result, anxiety levels can be high for perfectionists. If you are a perfectionist dissertation writer, in particular one who has never undertaken such a huge high-stakes writing project before, anxiety can be especially troublesome. You know that the quality of your written document will determine whether you graduate, and therefore possibly whether you will later be hired or promoted in a job. How do you know if what you have written is good enough, particularly if you don't submit drafts regularly to supervisors or get detailed feedback? For those supervisors who themselves have perfectionist tendencies, how do they manage their own writing? How do such supervisors decide whether what they write is good enough? How then do they decide when what their students write is good enough and so advise them that it is time to stop? How can dissertation writers make themselves stop, when the specter of an "imperfect dissertation" that will be evaluated by their superiors hangs over them? It is challenging for any of us who write to let go of revising and rewriting if our writing might not seem good enough. But sometimes time has run out and we must move on (see Chapter 10). We cannot wish perfectionism away, but perhaps can come to understand it so that it does not derail progress in the midst of our writing or, if we are supervisors, mislead students that we are working with into thinking they must follow a mythical model of perfection.

Characterizing a "Perfect" Dissertation

I think that everyone knows at some level that there is no such thing as a "perfect" dissertation, and that supervisors themselves probably can't or didn't write their own perfect master's theses or doctoral dissertations or expect their students to do so. Another side of us, whether student or supervisor, suspects that there might be such a thing. At the very least, the perfect dissertation will follow the university dissertation template exactly, adopt an accepted and admired research design and theoretical framework for the particular project, demonstrate deep and thorough knowledge of the relevant literature, present interesting and possibly innovative findings and conclusions, be competently if not beautifully written, contain no typos or grammar mistakes, and display a perfectly formatted reference list that is not missing any cited readings. A dissertation writer only has to go to the library or go online to view finished dissertations to get a sense of what "perfection" might look like, because in their finished polished form, they all look perfect at first glance. Not only do they look gorgeous, but supervisors have signed off on the finished document, so it must have reached an acceptable standard of competence, if not perfection. Looking at a finished dissertation can be both enlightening and intimidating. I suggest keeping your eye out for typos to make yourself feel better. There is bound to be at least one, as there was in mine.

Maybe there are some perfect dissertations, but most are not. And though some do, few doctoral dissertations win awards. They pass, so in that sense they are perfect in their adequacy. But passing means that they are good enough, not necessarily perfect. The problem is that you probably don't know, without the help of savvy supervisors, when your drafts are good enough. Moreover, once you reach this "perfectly adequate" stage, one in which your competence if not your brilliance is displayed, you must look ahead to having your dissertation drafts evaluated by one or more other dissertation committee members at a defense (viva, in the British system). My supervisor might find my draft adequate, but what about these other committee members? Uncertainty can loom large at this stage. Such concerns can easily derail you in the midst of otherwise productive writing sessions. Those of you who have perfectionist tendencies can become masters of procrastination.

Perfectionism as the Mother of Procrastination

Interested readers might want to read this section in conjunction with Chapter 8. In that chapter, I speculate on distractions that can derail dissertation writers from their goal of writing regularly until their dissertation drafts are completed. Procrastination is just one way that you can derail yourselves, but I include this malady in this chapter because various kinds of perfectionism and writing anxiety can tempt you into postponing the writing and revising that still need to be done until other "preparatory" things get done, such as more (and more, and more) reading. Fear of failure runs high in the lives of some dissertation writers, so at the time, procrastination can feel like a survival technique. An unfinished dissertation can be viewed as a postponed one, not as a failed, if completed, one.

Of course, some of you will also procrastinate just to avoid what you find to be the onerous task of serious writing, given that there are many more pleasant, or perhaps just useful, things to do. As expressed by Onwuegbuzie and Collins (2001, p. 562): "Academic procrastination has been associated with both fear of failure and task aversiveness." In an anecdote about procrastination among PhD students, Kearns, Gardiner, and Marshall (2008, p. 77; italics in original) tell a story of the "secret life of the PhD student." The story may sound familiar to many dissertation writers as well as to post-dissertation writers who are working on articles and books:

> You're sitting at your desk ready to start writing; it's 9.30 a.m. You think, "I'll just check my emails for 10 minutes and then I'll get started on my literature review." You open up your email and find there's one from your supervisor asking if your draft is ready. You quickly send it to the trash and check the next one. [...] It's 10.15 a.m. "Well," you think, "I may as well just get the rest of these emails cleared"; [...]; interesting reference from co-supervisor—send back saying thanks, and go look up reference—feel very satisfied when found, printed, stapled and put in pile with 40 other articles. It is now 11.00 a.m. "Well, it's been a busy morning, surely it's time for a cup of coffee." [the story continues describing the rest of the day, with nothing done]

Email and other distractions related to addictive social media surely must have been invented by the Gods of Procrastination. Not too long ago, we could at least reap some benefit from certain procrastination techniques that social media does not afford us: Apartments got cleaned, cooking and laundry got done, exercise happened, dogs got walked, and so on. Now we just sit tapping away at our computers or our hand-held devices, giving the impression to onlookers that we are working hard when in fact we have become sucked into the black hole of social media and internet hyperlinks. In all cases, however, procrastination activities slow down your progress to the point where the vision of the finished dissertation is like the vanishing point in a work of art—it extends to infinity. For the perfectionist, this distant vision is deadly because it can never be reached. But universities and supervising faculty reach a point at which they tell students their official time in the program is running out. Among others who have written about this dilemma, Kearns, Gardiner, and Marshall (2008) felt compelled to get their PhD students through their program fast, in response to internal and external pressures from the university and the workforce, in this case, in Australia. Under such pressure, there is no time for perfection, even if we believe it exists. And there comes a point in the midst of dissertation writing that there is also no more time for procrastination.

In my own PhD program, I felt no such pressure until I was trying to finish up a full draft of the dissertation. With three years of course work finished and another three years of dissertation work still in progress but nearing the end, I had moved home to finish writing. Because I worked on my writing nearly every day, I did not feel as though I was procrastinating, at least not in the style of the student in the Kearns et al. anecdote. But progress was slow. I was teaching part time, and I was in no rush to finish. To be honest, I would have been happy to actively procrastinate and stretch out the writing process another couple of years. In spite of the frustrations of writing, it was a delicious time in my life, intellectually rewarding, filled with the comforts of my own home, and replete with not just the pleasures of sporadic writing and regular teaching, but also with opportunities to escape on a daily basis for a walk to town for shopping or a walk on the beach for "essential" thinking time. I managed to write for some hours nearly every day on this schedule. When my advisers moved to a new university on the other side of the country and gave me a deadline (firm) if I wished to continue working with them, I was shocked. My slow if steady writing progress had to turn into fast writing progress or I would lose my advisers. Unhappily, I complied.

My brand of procrastination was not deeply linked to perfectionism, even though I could always find more to do on every chapter of my dissertation draft. It was linked partly to my ignorance of what was "good enough," and partly to the pleasures of my life at the time. Working in relative isolation at the end of my doctoral years, I did not know what perfectionism meant in doctoral dissertation writing, and forged ahead as best I could with some guidance from my two advisers. I actually felt I was being productive because I was working on some aspect of the dissertation nearly every day. So how could I be procrastinating? However, the literature on doctoral dissertation writing points to other self-sabotaging reasons for perfectionism and procrastination suffered by many dissertation writers that are less benign and that I discuss in the next section: fear of failure, fear of criticism and of not being able to live up to expectations, and self-sabotaging behaviors that seem designed to function as self-fulfilling prophecies. Thanks either to my age or my ignorance, I escaped many of these fears, but others do not. Note that the reasons I discuss in this chapter for some students' slow progress on dissertation writing differ somewhat from the "distractions" that I discuss in Chapter 8.

More Self-Sabotaging Behaviors and Attitudes

Perfectionist tendencies do not function in isolation from other attitudes that can lead to procrastination and other behaviors designed as escape mechanisms from the pressures and deadlines of actual dissertation writing. Here are some:

Fear of Failure

Some people no doubt feel more anxious than do others at the thought of failing at high-stakes tasks, for reasons too deeply psychological for me to cover in depth here. For readers who fit this description and who feel that their fears are debilitating, I suggest they seek resources other than this book for exploring the causes and cures. Suffice it to say that for any of us who are undertaking a challenging high-stakes task for the first time, it is impossible to know what success feels like, because the task has not been completed yet. If we do not know what success feels like, then fear of failure, or at least some anxiety about failing, seems completely normal. I might worry about a doctoral student who has no such fears, wondering if he or she knows what lies ahead. Particularly in the case of students who truly need the doctoral degree for professional reasons (to get or keep a job, for example), anxiety about possibly failing to complete the dissertation is a rational response to the challenge. The question then becomes—will fear of failure motivate you to complete the dissertation, or paralyze you into inaction, unrealistic goals of perfection, and withdrawal from the doctoral program? If you are a student who is experiencing fear of failure, are you reflecting on your fears, either privately or with trusted others, and linking fears to perfectionist tendencies or to other possible causes? Such reflection, expressed in personal journals or in communication with others, can help dissertation writers move ahead in spite of your fears.

Resistance to Criticism

It is probably safe to say that all of us love positive feedback on our writing, feedback that lavishes us with praise at our extraordinary ideas, immaculate research design and analysis, and elegant writing. I am trying to remember even a single time when I got such feedback, or gave it, for that matter, at least in a form unaccompanied by critical commentary. Positive commentary helps writers keep their spirits up and feeds their motivation to continue working, and most writing instructors and dissertation supervisors probably do not provide enough of it, myself included. Nevertheless, the purpose of critical feedback is, after all, not just to point out aspects of a piece of writing that work well, but also to identify areas that need to be improved and provide suggestions for doing so, without setting up an unrealistic goal of perfection.

Two forms of resistance to criticism can slow down your dissertation writing. The first response happens when low-confidence dissertation writers link critical commentary to evaluations of themselves as people. Critical commentary you receive on your dissertation work thus becomes a critique of the self, not just of the writing project. "I am not good enough," rather than "This current draft is not yet good enough." Some supervisors, and some manuscript reviewers for journal article submissions too, might not craft the wording of critical commentary in ways designed to encourage a writer while simultaneously critiquing an idea, a phrasing, or an interpretation.

The other kind of resistance to critique happens if you are a dissertation writer who is <u>over</u>-confident in what you have done. Such dissertation writers will not trust the suggestions from others, who in their minds cannot possibly know as much as they do. It is true that supervisors sometimes know much less about your research topics than you yourselves have come to know. However, unless the supervisors are complete novices at the job of supervising, they know a lot more about all other aspects of what it takes to carry out and complete a dissertation project. If you are a dissertation writer who fears or resists critical commentary from knowledgeable supervisors, you risk losing valuable opportunities to move your thinking and writing forward. And beware: It is easy for some writers in the midst of their writing to hide from supervisors for fear of critical feedback.

The Burden of "Shoulds"

This section discusses some details of what I introduced earlier as the "should disease," in which dissertation writers feel compelled to aim for perfection by following prescriptions, templates, how-to guides, and advice by experts. Such guides are compelling, because most dissertation writers have never done a project like a dissertation before and so welcome some guidance. After all, there are indeed many things you should know and do. How-to guide books for L1 and L2 dissertation writers and supervisors have been around for a long time and offer prescriptions for time management, daily writing patterns such as word minimums and time-on-task, order of writing, and strategies for doing research and for sharing writing and revising (Becker, 1986; Bitchener, 2010; McAlpine & Amundsen, 2011; Murray & Beglar, 2009; Paltridge & Starfield, 2007, 2019; Sternberg, 1981). As useful as these suggestions are, I want to emphasize here that you need to identify your own obstacles and then devise strategies for getting your writing done, which may or may not follow advice provided in guidebooks or by supervisors.

If you are a dissertation writer who is encumbered by "shoulds" and "should nots," you are also probably encumbered by guilt for not getting things done on the "should" list and for doing things on the "should not" list. These lists can be long and daunting, as the partial list that follows indicates.

For example, dissertation writers *should* have read enough by the time they start writing to have developed some idea of what others have done on their topic; they *should* make notes on their readings and keep their notes in some kind of systematic order; they *should* have designed a study and carried it out according to accepted procedures; they *should* have all their participant consent forms done and signed; they *should* begin writing early in the project and not wait till all their data are collected; they *should* cite all their sources; they *should* put quote marks around and page numbers with cited strings of words; they *should* hire a language editor if their writing needs polishing that they cannot do themselves; they *should* make a realistic plan for finishing their writing; they *should* try to complete their projects in a timely manner; they *should* do what they can to stay healthy. In general they *should* follow their university's guidelines and templates for dissertation writing. Too many shoulds! But wait.

Don't forget the "should nots." Here are a few:

Dissertation writers *should not* plagiarize; they *should not* wait until the last minute to write; they *should not* depend on their supervisors for everything; they *should not* collect all their data and start writing before a proposal has been approved; they *should not* go for long stretches without doing anything on their dissertations; they *should not* hire someone to write their dissertations for them; they *should not* translate work from another language and present it as their own; they *should not* reject critical feedback from knowledgeable readers; they *should not* reveal the identities of participants who need or wish to remain anonymous; they *should not* lose sleep over missing deadlines; they *should not* make feeble excuses for not getting writing done according to the schedule they laid out for themselves; *should not* not try to follow contradictory suggestions about their writing; they *should not* lose so much sleep or surround themselves with so much stress that they cannot function or maintain a healthy relationship with loved ones.

As sensible as these "should" and "should not" lists are, they are also quite overwhelming. The lists need to be seen for what they are: Except for strict conventions about plagiarizing, most of these are not rules, but reasonable, commonsense ideas to be followed or not. Guilt awaits those who are overburdened by shoulds and should nots, and unresolved guilt will not allow you to focus on your writing!

Writer's Block

Among other negative consequences of perfectionism is a final malady I will discuss in this chapter: the phenomenon of writer's block. Writer's block is a type of paralysis experienced by some perfectionist writers who feel they just can't "get it right," and that what they do is never good enough. These responses to one's own high-stakes writing are actually quite normal, as long as they do not permanently block you from moving ahead with your work. Writer's block and advice for stalled writers have long been written about, but mostly from the perspective of creative and literary writers and writers in undergraduate composition studies (Rose, 1980, 1984, 1985; Sommers, 2006). However, research writers and academics experience similar blocks (Ahern & Manathunga, 2004; Lu, 2015). In the case of dissertation writers, blocks can stem from pressures I have discussed in this chapter, such as perfectionism, exacerbated by writers' feeling overwhelmed at the enormous and high-stakes nature of the project, fear of criticism, fear of failure, insidious comparisons with others, lack of confidence writing in both L1 and L2, a host of personal issues, and general insecurities. Here are a few examples of blocks experienced by some dissertation writers:

- constantly changing the topic or planned work
- avoiding all forms of communication with the supervisor

- isolating themselves from the department and from other students
- and avoiding submitting work for review. (Ahern & Manathunga, 2004, p. 238)

This chapter doesn't provide tricks or cures for blocks that might stem from perfectionism, but aims to help you understand your blocks and the relation between blocks and perfectionist tendencies, and to help your supervisors understand the blocks that you might be experiencing. One of my doctoral students who was working on her dissertation at the time wrote me about her very sensible attitude toward blocks: "Blocks are always around the corner—I feel the key is to have strategies that work for when they show up. One of my strategies is to give in sometimes. I just accept that I can't do it and it's natural that I have blocks like I have blocks in life!" (Mayumi Asaba, September 1, 2017). Giving in to a block (we hope a temporary one) does not mean settling for inferior writing on the dissertation, but adjusting one's priorities and expectations. It is likely that those of you who are experiencing blocks can come to understand them, and so devise strategies for dealing with them, even if it means giving in to them for the time, as Mayumi did. To repeat a message in this chapter, the perfect dissertation does not exist—this attitude alone can help prevent blocks.

SUMMARY OF MAIN POINTS

1. Dissertation writers with perfectionist tendencies might have trouble completing their projects.
2. Self-sabotaging behaviors of many kinds can obstruct progress on dissertation writing.
3. Recognizing self-sabotaging behaviors can help dissertation writers develop strategies for combatting them.

SUGGESTIONS FOR DISCUSSION AND REFLECTION

1. To what extent do you consider yourself a perfectionist or a realist?
2. How do you know if what you have written on your dissertation draft is "good enough"? Be as specific as possible in your discussion with fellow dissertation writers.
3. Are you troubled by any self-sabotaging behaviors or tendencies in your dissertation writing, including perfectionism? What are these and where do they come from? How can you combat them?
4. If you suspect that there might be something like a "perfect dissertation," what would this be like? If you believe there is no such thing as a perfect dissertation, explain your reasoning.
5. Have you ever suffered from writer's block during dissertation writing? What do you believe caused this and how did you handle it?

Chapter 5

Staying Healthy

"I don't have time to take care of myself properly. I have to finish writing my dissertation by a deadline."

This chapter discusses the importance of staying healthy during dissertation writing, on the assumption that good physical and mental health will help dissertation writers stay mentally sharp, physically strong enough to persist in challenging tasks and long writing sessions, and sociable enough to reach out to others for help if needed. Although this view seems like uncontroversial common sense, it is a lot to ask of dissertation writers, particularly those who are on strict deadlines and so perceive that they have no time for anything but the dissertation.

Common health issues suffered by dissertation writers at this high-pressure stage of writing result from neglect of self, stress, lack of sleep, and overwork because they think they simply have no time to take better care of themselves. Excessive hours of sitting at a computer lead to aches, pains, and other physical discomforts. Sleep-deprived dissertation writers get sick more easily than those who manage enough sleep, and once sick, might continue working through nose-blowing, fevers, coughs, and body aches and so prolong an illness. Emotional health can suffer, too, if stresses are not relieved by social support and by relaxing standards of perfection that are too high (see Chapter 4). I am describing some of the dissertation writers I have known, who in the throes of high-pressure dissertation writing could not find ways to follow a healthy lifestyle. Perhaps the list of commonsense topics in this chapter will sound like wishful thinking to them. But I'll try. The topics include the importance of breaks, exercise, adequate sleep, decent food, vigilance for signs of trouble, and the courage to ask for help if needed. In general, the chapter asks dissertation writers to place priorities on health, rather than on finishing a chapter at any cost. This is not just pie-in-the-sky/roll-your-eyeballs advice. Dissertation writers who are healthy mentally and physically can probably write twice as much in half the time as those who are physical and mental wrecks. Imagine: twice as much in half the time!

A Few Personal Reflections First

In *Before the Dissertation*, I discussed briefly some quality of life issues as students prepare for dissertation writing, including health. I expand on some of the health issues in this chapter, first because they are especially important while you are in the midst of writing, but also because doctoral students tend to be more isolated at this stage and less connected to colleagues, friends, faculty, and family than they are during course work and proposal writing (see Chapter 7, Loneliness and Isolation). All these people in your dissertation writing world might notice oddities in your social lives, diet, sleep patterns, exercise, and physical and emotional well-being and thus be able to remind you to get back into a healthier lifestyle, one that in the long run will result in greater productivity and better quality work. I have noticed such oddities and lapses in myself and in some of my own doctoral students, and colleagues have related stories of their own dissertation writing days that point to the hazards awaiting those who focus single-mindedly on non-stop writing. Such dissertation writers don't intentionally wish to harm their health of course, and they probably understand at some level the connections between good health and an active brain. But driven by deadlines and once into a flow state (Csikszentmihalyi, 1990) of writing, you can easily forgo meals, sleep, exercise, and even bathing. (Yuck.) International graduate students and L2 speakers of English as well as L1 English users may not be fully aware of how central physical and mental health is to finishing their dissertations in a timely way.

For the most part, I did not fall into such extreme patterns. Yes, I sat at my desk or table for long hours, feeling stiff and disoriented when I finally resurfaced, but I learned that my brain was not a friend to me after more than five or six hours of writing. This is still the case today. My days are planned so that I do not push myself into a stupor of writing. I also never write at night, finding that my brain, activated during writing episodes, requires several hours of down time before I can sleep. Without sufficient sleep, I can do very little productive writing beyond the mechanical tasks, which of course also need to get done (see Chapter 6). Since my dissertation writing days, in the interest of decent sleep and a brain that will get me through the next day, I also avoid caffeine except in the mornings, alcohol after dinner, and uppers or downers designed to give me artificial energy or fake sleep (see the section on Substances). And even during the throes of dissertation writing, I managed to exercise every day by inventing something I needed to buy at a store in town and walking there and back as fast as I could manage or reading drafts and walking at the same time. Don't get me wrong—I am no master of discipline or will power. I could never manage to take regular breaks that experts say are essential, and I took longer than most people to finish my dissertation. These behaviors were the survival techniques I could manage at the time and that I still follow for the most part. I turn into an intellectual and physical slug without them, and frequent breaks distract me, despite what some experts recommend (see the discussion below of the Pomodoro technique). I don't think I am unique in this regard even though the details for each of you will differ.

Food figures in too. Although I have never been much of a snacker and am positively repelled at the sight and smell of Cheetos, I noticed that during dissertation work, my daily post-prandial cookie or two (rich white chocolate macadamia nut treats...) caused a significant dip in my energy later in the afternoon. Of course they did. We can all read these days about the effects of sugary fatty snacks on the glucose levels in our blood, but the best lesson for me was to experience these sugar highs and lows. It was my own body, not my will power, beginning at the dissertation writing stage, that shifted my diet toward one that I could write a health-food book on: vegetables, fruits, salads, nuts, poultry and fish, and, over the years, fewer and fewer sugars and starches. I can tell that the gradual reduction (not elimination, unfortunately) of the "bad" things has also reduced my cravings for them and also keeps my brain active for most of the day.

The question for myself that I cannot answer (the experiment cannot be done at this point) is whether I would have had the will power to adjust my diet had my body not reacted badly to certain things. To this day, I have watched myself occasionally consume a basket of sweet potato fries or a chocolate chip cookie the size of a small dinner plate without being able to stop. I do not know where the will power comes from to control cravings for such addictive and sinful foods, and so do not know how to effectively advise doctoral writers that I work with. For weak-willed dissertation writers who have such cravings, I can only suggest that you monitor your intake of sinful foods and how they affect you, and keep nothing in the house on the sinful list that affects you adversely. Your active brain will thank you. And for people who associate breaks from dissertation work (essential, in some views) with sinful dips into sinful foods (tempting but not essential), I hope your will power is stronger than mine. (I wonder if anyone has ever done a correlational study on the relationship between the consumption of white chocolate macadamia nut cookies and dissertation writing productivity....)

In what follows, I discuss the need for dissertation writers to maintain health by taking breaks, exercising, sleeping enough, eating well, avoiding nasty substances, managing stress, and above all staying vigilant. I hope readers will forgive me if I come across sounding too smug or didactic, particularly since I am not an ideal role model; please know that I have not achieved all that I write about. Feel free to move on to another chapter if you feel this one doesn't pass the smug test.

Breaks

When I was writing my dissertation, no one told me about the importance of taking regular breaks during long writing sessions. Either that, or I didn't pay attention to this advice. Even now, many years later, I do not follow this advice much, and end up spending several hours sitting in a comfortable chair with my gaze alternating between the computer screen and the cypress tree outside the library window. My writing sessions last two or three hours at a time but for potty breaks. I know that for maximum mental and physical health, people need to take breaks from intensive work such as dissertation writing and other important writing, but I cannot seem to make myself do this, for fear of losing my "flow" state, if I am lucky enough to be in one. This is partly because I tend to interpret breaks as interruptions. Interruptions disturb my concentration, and because I am sometimes easily distracted, I need to find ways to prevent such interruptions. My sense has long been that for mental health and well-being, I should improve my ability to focus, concentrate, and work in uninterrupted sessions. Some years ago I read Csikszentmihalyi's (1990) book on *Flow* with interest and his view that "optimal psychological experience" is achieved in flow states. I found that indeed some of my most productive writing sessions have happened in flow states, when I lose track of time and work without interruption. It is difficult for me to imagine that enforced breaks could possibly benefit my ability to concentrate. How is it possible to work in short spurts and still maintain focus? But there is an opposing view, probably healthier than mine.

I only recently learned about the "Pomodoro Technique" (Cirillo, 2006) for enforcing breaks on oneself and so apparently promoting maximum efficiency in how people accomplish tasks such as studying and writing (thanks, Tiara, for alerting me to this work). Yes, there are frequent breaks in this technique, but these breaks are not interpreted as distractions or interruptions. The technique uses a timer (originally a "tomato" kitchen timer, hence the "Pomodoro" name) to strictly divide the activities of studying and writing into 25-minute sessions separated by short breaks, and then slightly longer sessions with slightly longer breaks. The technique apparently forces people to concentrate intensely during the short study sessions in ways they may have trouble doing without the schedule. According to the originator, Francesco Cirillo, who developed this technique during his university days as he observed his own distractions and inefficient ways of studying, time needed to become an ally, not an enemy (Cirillo, p. 1). If we feel constantly pressed for time—that there is not enough of it, that we are not using it efficiently, that it will run out—we can easily become so anxious about time disappearing that we become derailed in achieving our goals. Cirillo has made the point that with enforced and regular short breaks, anxiety about time disappears and motivation and concentration improve. In this technique, breaks are not seen as interruptions.

This argument makes sense, but I don't know if it would work for all writers. I have yet to try this technique, perhaps because I do not often suffer from a time anxiety problem, nor do I often feel that time passes during writing sessions without my having accomplished anything. Something always gets done. I also do get up and down frequently, look out the window as I write, and avoid setting daily writing goals that I cannot possibly reach. During my dissertation writing days, my own brain dictated how long I could sit at my worktable: Five hours a day was about my maximum in those more intense and youthful days. But for those who do suffer from time anxiety, which many dissertation writers likely do, the Pomodoro technique or a similar technique of enforced writing and enforced breaks to improve concentration might be worth trying.

Other sources of anxiety such as lack of confidence in yourself as a writer and inadequate feelings of self-efficacy in writing can be even more disruptive than anxiety about time (Huerta, Goodson, Beigi, & Chlup, 2017). As Huerta et al., noted, "self-efficacy is important for academic writing because the activity tends to be self-scheduled and performed alone" (p. 717). At the dissertation writing stage, your ability to be productive in solitary conditions requires that you sustain your confidence and manage your anxiety without the regular contact with others that you had during course work.

In general, anxiety of any kind does not make for productive writing sessions or contribute to overall health, and can seriously affect how productive you are in your writing. In fact, any technique that prevents or reduces writing anxiety and that improves your focus and confidence during dissertation writing is worth trying.

Exercise

Exercise is one of those strategic activities during dissertation writing that can potentially reduce anxiety and improve concentration. However, a lot of people don't exercise. I know that. This group includes people who just don't like to exercise (my mother was one of those; she preferred to read novels and smoke) and others who claim they just don't have time to fit exercise in to their dissertation writing schedules. Some people also mistakenly believe that "to exercise" means to take a chunk of time out of the day to go to a gym, to jog or swim, or to walk for an hour alone or with a group, and then after any of these activities to shower and change clothes. These activities take time.

Exercise can indeed mean any of these things, but it can also mean just 20 or 30 minutes a day, or even every other day, of doing something involving movement beyond that of fingers on a keyboard. My friend Merrill has a stationary bicycle in her house, so even in the depths of a Toronto winter she can get her muscles working and her circulation going. If you drive to your university and find a parking lot that forces you to walk 10 minutes to get to your office, you have reached your 20 minutes per day. If you have a dog and let it take you on a walk every day, you have done the same. Combining reading and thinking with exercise may not suit everyone, but those who can read and/or think while walking or using a treadmill will never feel as though they are robbing themselves of time that contributes to dissertation writing. Such combinations of activities allow you to ponder writing problems, plan what to do next, or review what has been done. In my case, the nearest market and the school library are both about 20 minutes away from my home, so a daily walk there and back achieves four goals in one: food shopping, thinking-reading time as I walk, writing time at the library, and exercise.

In short, bodily strength and good circulation affect the brain. This is not a controversial statement. And an active brain is needed for dissertation writing.

No more needs to be said.

Sleep

Listen to how odd this statement sounds: I am too busy to sleep; I'll catch up tomorrow.

Sleep can be elusive for dissertation writers. But with good sleep and other good habits, you can accomplish twice as much in half the time, as I mentioned earlier in the chapter. You are also less likely to get sick than those who work through the night. Look on any website under "the importance of sleep" and you will confirm what we all know—that good sleep is necessary for physical health, weight control, mental productivity, and memory. It is also a myth that you can catch up on days of lost sleep with one or two 10-hour nights. It just doesn't work that way. The only way to recover health and mental acuity is to sleep enough hours regularly every night (Webster, 2008).

But if you are in the midst of dissertation writing, it can be difficult to stop writing if you are on a roll or if you have a strict deadline to get a chapter to your supervisor. Just another hour of writing, you say to yourself, as midnight approaches. And after midnight, "just another couple of paragraphs to finish this section." Then at 3 AM, bug-eyed with fatigue, you finally roll into bed, unable to sleep because you are too wired. If this happens to you, be sure to re-read what you wrote during the sleepless periods before you submit it to your supervisor: It could be incomprehensible drivel spewed out by your fatigued brain.

I envy people who are good sleepers. Knowing what I do about the benefits of good sleep, I am distressed that my brain does not leave me pleasantly unconscious for longer than it does, particularly when I have nothing much to fret about at this stage of my career. So even though I don't write at night, I also don't sleep well some nights, and then struggle to write efficiently and creatively the next day. Dissertation writers, like all writers, really do need to find ways to balance productive writing with sufficient good-quality sleep. (I do not count as "good-quality sleep" that which is induced by pills or alcohol.) I don't have good answers about how to do this, except to keep this goal in mind during the entire dissertation writing process, and to avoid catastrophizing about perceived lack of progress, to the extent possible. If you are a dissertation writer who tells yourself that something catastrophic will happen if you don't finish another section or write for another two hours, you will surely miss out on needed sleep, a decision for which you will pay dearly later.

Food

Another commonsense assertion is that what you eat affects how your brain works. One does not have to be a rocket scientist to know that sweets and carbohydrates provide a short-term boost to energy, and that other foods such as vegetables, fruits, fish, poultry, and walnuts provide long-term boosts (Harvard Health Publishing, n.d.). In the midst of dissertation writing, you need long-term boosts that improve concentration, memory, and mental and physical energy. As good as the short-term boosts might feel at the moment, such as those triggered by my beloved white chocolate chip macadamia nut cookies that I wrote about earlier in this chapter, they don't last. A brain crash is inevitable, and dissertation writers can't afford too many brain crashes. The long-term boosts to your memory and productivity, on the other hand, will come from fatty fish, vegetables and fruits, beans, and whole grains. (My apologies to readers who are rolling their eyes at this point, at such prescriptive yet commonsense statements.)

I am not sure how pervasive this habit is for dissertation writers, but some writers do skip meals, and instead keep bowls and boxes of snacks next to their computer to stave off hunger. Often such snacks take the form of crackers, chips, and sweets. An argument can be made that such convenient foods are ideal, because you do not need to get up to prepare meals or wash dishes, unless you are in the unenviable position of being both a dissertation writer and a parent and/or spouse (Lillis & Curry, 2018; Mewburn, 2019b). Also, for PhD students on a tight budget, these snacks can be cheap. If you are a doctoral student who is tempted by such conveniences, and one who chooses to write ten hours a day to the exclusion of sleep, exercise, and real meals, you may end up with a dissertation draft a year later. However, if you look in the mirror at the conclusion of your dissertation writing, you will probably see a haggard pasty face, circles under your eyes, and a bloated physique that you don't recognize. So don't skip meals, live on Cup Noodles ramen, or snack on Cheetos. If you must snack, try carrots or nuts.

This depiction might be an exaggeration of course, but my point remains—dissertation writers need quick and active brains along with physical energy to read, think, and write efficiently and effectively. Short-term boosts may feel good at the moment, but they can lead to long-term inefficiency.

Substances

By "substances," I refer to prescription or over-the-counter products designed to relieve pain, induce sleep, keep you alert the next day, combat depression, reduce anxiety, or promote euphoria and a sense of well-being. For some students, alcohol is used for some of these purposes, and licit and illicit drugs for other students. I don't know what the situation is in other countries in the world, but in the United States, a visit to a doctor by highly stressed dissertation writers with the rather normal complaints of anxiety and depression can result in students' walking out of the doctor's office with one or more high-potency prescriptions for tranquilizers, anti-depressants, or pain relievers. Such prescriptions may or may not be addictive. It pays to read the fine print and ask a lot of questions. Among graduate students themselves, whether domestic or international, there will also likely be lore about what substances help you avoid panic, stay awake, sleep better, or boost your brain power. In all cases, legal substances can be used with care or abused, and illegal substances can get you expelled from the university or worse.

In the interest of staying healthy during dissertation writing, it pays to ask, "What do I want?" versus "What do I need?" in the short term and the long term. The answers will differ for each question. And no substance except perhaps good food will actually help you write your dissertation over the long term.

Stress Is Hazardous to Your Health

Stress, burnout, and other negative feelings "can impair student wellbeing, and consequently, stymie dissertation productivity" (Russell-Pinson & Harris, 2019, p. 63; see also Chapter 3). Stress is probably the most insidious of all the health hazards related to dissertation writing because it tends to be invisible or can easily be disguised as something else. Some symptoms of stress during dissertation writing that can be misinterpreted as other things include: digestive problems attributed to poor diet, headaches thought to result from an outdated eyeglass prescription, mid-life acne, poor sleep ostensibly due to ambient noise, frequent colds said to be caused by contact with other cold sufferers not just from a lowered immune system, neck and back problems thought to result from poor posture rather than from muscle tension, and memory and concentration problems mistakenly attributed to aging. Some of these ailments, Russell-Pinson and Harris (2019,

p. 68) remind us, "such as head-aches and back problems, might not be seen as stress-related, but at times will be experienced as a proxy for emotional distress." But all of these ailments can be connected to the stress of dissertation writing, particularly if the writing is not going smoothly or if you are facing impossible deadlines. If you are also caught in the midst of conflicting demands of work, family, and dissertation writing (Levecque, Anseel, De Beuckelaer, Van der Heyden, & Gisle, 2017), concentration suffers, anxiety increases, depression lurks, emotions turn fragile, and the possibility of giving up looms.

Stress experienced during dissertation writing might not stem just from factors in L1 and L2 writers' immediate academic and family lives or be connected in clear ways to actual dissertation writing. It might also be exacerbated by financial strain, cultural and linguistic challenges across and within cultures, visa or lodging problems, homesickness, and lack of familiarity and experience with a project as enormous and overwhelming as writing a doctoral dissertation (Russell-Pinson & Harris, 2019). What Straforini (2015) calls "non-traditional students" (such as first generation graduate students, students with financial problems or gaps in their educations, adult students unused to not being in full control of their lives) might be especially susceptible to debilitating stresses during dissertation writing, particularly if practical suggestions (such as time management) do not work for them. How can both you and your dissertation supervisor learn to attend to the many sometimes subtle signs that something is wrong, particularly if a university does not host dissertation writing support groups or provide professional writing support of the type recommended by Russell-Pinson and Harris (2019)?

Maybe it is not possible for you to eliminate stress in your lives during your dissertation writing stage, but it is possible to recognize its sources and to take steps to alleviate it where possible—or as Sosin and Thomas (2014) say, in their harrowing case study of "Karl," to "manage" it. Stress, these authors point out, arises when what doctoral students are required to do exceeds their capacity and when they come to see themselves as victims, as Karl did. However, stress is not always negative or debilitating. Positive stress can spur you on, "be beneficial as it awakens in the doctoral student increased attentiveness to tasks, scholarship, excellence, and progress," and help them cross the "finish line," unlike "*distress*" (p. 56, italics in original). The challenge is how to remain vigilant about the sources of and solutions to stress during the writing stage before real burnout sets in. Positive consequences for mental and physical health will follow from such vigilance, which I comment on in this last section.

Vigilance

I end this chapter with a note about the need for all of you in the midst of dissertation writing to stay vigilant about your health. Again, my comments reflect common sense and do not require references to scientific and medical literature for support, though there is plenty of literature out there for those of you who need documented evidence. Staying vigilant about your health requires only that you pay attention to your body and brain during the dissertation writing time, when stress and anxiety are inevitable. You know when your body and brain are not functioning at full capacity because you probably can't write or think well. You may easily get sick or suffer from debilitating mood swings. It could be especially difficult at such a time to realize precise causes and to seek help. As Turley (2013) noted in his blog, graduate students who are "suffering terribly from depression or anxiety may not seek any help because of denial that they have a serious issue or because they are ashamed." You also may not link physical and mental health, but there is a correlational if not causal relationship. Equally dangerous for L2 dissertation writers studying outside your home cultures is feeling that you don't know where to go for help or that some stigma is attached to admitting you have physical or mental health problems. All I can say at this point is: Pay attention to the signs as you are writing your dissertation. Here are some of them:

If your neck and shoulders and lower back hurt, this is evidence that you need to move more and take more breaks (stretch, walk) and possibly change how and where you sit (or stand) to write. If your eyes bother you, it is time to consider the lighting in your work space, get a vision check, adjust the brightness of your computer screen, and take breaks in which you close your eyes or shift to a long distance focus outside a window or on a walk. If you feel weak, sluggish, or lack mental acuity, it is time to look at your diet, your sleep patterns, and your intake of various substances. If you feel wired and hyperactive and can't sleep, this is a signal that a number of things might need to be changed, including exercise routines, the times of day or night that you write, your choices of food and drink and other substances, and your basic attitude toward your dissertation writing. If you feel burned out, it might be because you are, and so need to reflect on your situation and maybe seek some counseling. All of these aspects of taking care of your health during dissertation writing influence how quickly and efficiently your brain will work, and so how quickly and efficiently your dissertation will get written. This kind of vigilance aims at a long-term perspective, with a long-term goal in mind, which is what is needed during dissertation writing.

In other words, dissertation writing is not just about the physical activity of writing. It requires the foundational participation of your brain and your body, both of which require breaks, exercise, sleep, good food, no substance abuse, and vigilance that all is working well.

But What to Share with Your Supervisor?

The question about how much your dissertation supervisor needs to know about your health while you are in the process of writing, and how much guidance on health issues dissertation writers might expect from supervisors, is a difficult one. I understand that both dissertation writers and supervisors might believe that the less that is known and said about the dissertation writer's health (or about the supervisor's health, for that matter) the better (see Chapter 3). It is easy for shared information about health to turn into lists of excuses you make for not getting your work done or for missing meetings or deadlines. Perhaps the best way for supervisors to alert students as to how important it is to stay healthy during dissertation writing is to talk to them or write them a memo as a group rather than singling a student out individually. However, those supervisors who are willing to be good listeners—and good role models—can maintain an open-door policy to individual students along with assurances of confidentiality. I think that both you and supervisors will know when shared health information is genuine or exaggerated, particularly when a relationship of trust exists between you. The most important thing for both you and supervisors to remember is that health must come first. Without it, a doctoral dissertation might not get finished.

However, when things are not working well, and if you are not able to share health issues with supervisors, you need to ask for help, somewhere. Universities often have health centers, counseling offices, and usually international student centers where L1 and L2 students can go for support and guidance (see Russell-Pinson & Harris, 2019). If there is no such center, then you can reach out to trusted friends, faculty, or family members, and either join or start a dissertation writing group with classmates. Trying to finish writing a dissertation at the expense of physical and mental health does not pay off in either the long or the short run.

SUMMARY OF MAIN POINTS

1. Attending to physical and emotional health needs to be a high priority in a dissertation writer's life.
2. Good food, good sleep, and exercise are fundamental to a dissertation writer's mental and physical energy and well-being.
3. Although it is easy to postpone attention to health when dissertation writers face deadlines, to do so can actually be counter-productive and impede completion.

SUGGESTIONS FOR DISCUSSION AND REFLECTION

1. To what extent do you pay attention to your health on a regular basis? Does your attention vacillate according to how busy you get with dissertation writing and other academic work?
2. Do you take breaks as you write? What do these consist of and are you satisfied with how the breaks work for you?
3. From what you have learned during your own dissertation writing about the role of a healthy life style as you work to complete your thesis, what advice do you have for doctoral students who have not yet started writing?
4. What changes, if any, would you like to make in your life style during your dissertation writing time? What is your reasoning behind your views?
5. Do you ever share any personal information about your health with your supervisor? What is your reasoning behind your decision to share or not to share information?

Chapter 6

Low- and High-IQ Days

"When we are emotionally upset or stressed, we can't think straight. The IQ points we need to thoughtfully consider decisions are depleted temporarily."

—Relly Nadler blog, *Psychology Today,* April 29, 2011

Everyone has what I call low- and high-IQ (Intelligence Quotient) days. Note that IQ tests as measures of intelligence have not been considered adequate for many decades, given the many kinds of intelligence that have been posited since the 1980s (Gardner, 1983; Sternberg, 1988, 1999) and the lack of agreement about whether there are even multiple intelligences or a single intelligence. I use the terms *high-IQ* and *low-IQ days* metaphorically, tongue-in-cheek, for humor and simplicity to make a point.

For any number of reasons, dissertation writers, like all of us, may go through a day, or days, when they feel as though they have no brain. Their thinking is foggy, their mental energy low, their writing (if they can manage any) labored. High-IQ days, on the other hand, are what we all hope for. On these days, high mental energy and quick and creative thinking lead to productive writing sessions and a sense of confidence in our abilities, both of which contribute to the motivation to continue writing the next day. In this chapter, I point out that dissertation writers can make both low- and high-IQ days work for them, thus alleviating the guilt and disappointment we all feel on low days. The kinds of tasks that writers do on low and high days differ, but both are necessary and productive. In fact, we should hope for enough low-IQ days during a major project to get the inevitable tedious work done without feeling like we are wasting our high-IQ days on the necessary but mindless mechanical tasks. The trick is not to force high-IQ tasks on ourselves on a low-IQ day, not to waste a high-IQ day on mechanical tasks, and to know some strategies for adjusting tasks to fit both kinds of days.

First, let me clarify that I use the terms high- and low-IQ metaphorically to indicate either feelings of high mental energy and alertness or of sluggishness, forgetfulness, and intellectual emptiness. No doubt we have all experienced both kinds of feelings. There may actually be negative consequences on the low days. For instance, most of us have been forced to take various kinds of tests in our school days at times when we were feeling intellectually and emotionally low, and noticed that such low, slow days adversely influenced our test performance even if we consider ourselves pretty good test takers (I don't). Similarly, my sense has always been that if we were to give people the same IQ (or other) test on a high and low day that the scores would be quite different. Besides, such tests cannot measure our competence for sustained work on long-term projects such as dissertations. The poorest test taker might write a brilliant monograph dissertation or collection of dissertation articles. Still, for dissertation writers, many of whom are on tight schedules, high and low days have consequences for what you get done and how efficiently and creatively you work on a daily basis, apart from your various kinds of intelligence and expertise (Gardner, 1983; Sternberg, 1999).

In what follows, I describe in more detail what these low and high days feel like, not because there is anything new in these descriptions, but in order to assure anxious dissertation writers how normal ups and downs are. Readers can add their own stories—they are endless. My points will be that all of us working on a major writing project need to know ourselves as writers and to work with, not against, what we know of ourselves, and that some kind of writing or writing-related activities can be done on both kinds of days.

Stories of Some Low-IQ Days

I recall dreading the low days, the days of feeling intellectually empty, whether from fatigue, illness, confusion, overwork, or anxiety, because I knew I could not get much writing done on those days. However, they are inevitable for most of us, and—the good news—usually temporary.

But the low days are hard to get through. One of the most distressing things for a writer who has a deadline on a high-stakes project like a thesis or dissertation is to wake up in the morning with no brain—a classic low-IQ day. In my case, I know the minute I open my eyes in the morning if I will have a high- or low-IQ that day, and I usually know why. My relatively infrequent low-IQ days are most often connected to poor quality sleep, and as someone who cannot nap (I have tried), I must face an entire day with sluggish foggy thinking (or as I might say on such a brainless day, sluggy foggish thinking). On such a day I have so little mental and physical energy that I am lucky to remember which computer file I must work on or to be able to force myself to exercise. I am forgetful on such days. More than is normal for all of us, I might think of something I need from another room, but once I get there, forget what I intended to do or retrieve. Or at the market, I wander around trying to remember what it was I needed, but because I also forgot to bring my shopping list, I have to hope that some item will visually trigger my memory. Also, as is the case for others, I believe, my IQ drops after a big lunch or after eating rich or sweet foods, as happened to me this afternoon. I do not regret the buckwheat crepe with salmon, pesto, mushroom, and carmelized onion that I ate about an hour ago—it was heavenly. But my productivity for the afternoon's writing has plummeted. I must find some mechanical work to do on this book project so that I can end the day of writing with some sense that I did not waste the afternoon. I'll come back to this chapter later. (Which I did. Many times.)

So it is absolutely normal for many of us to feel, on some writing days, mentally and physically slow and sluggish and heavy and empty and depressed and uncreative and bored/boring and fatigued and worthless and stupid and incompetent... Quite a list, which could no doubt be expanded. Moreover, each of these feelings could be presented on a nuanced continuum, from a little sluggish to extremely sluggish, or a little stupid to excessively stupid. If you happen to be the kind of person who has never experienced such days, then you have my permission to skip to another chapter, but I urge you to continue reading as a way to comprehend what your less fortunate students, classmates, colleagues, and professors sometimes go through. You might be able to offer encouragement.

Part of knowing oneself as a writer is understanding the characteristics of our particular low-IQ days, and knowing something about what causes them. In my case, as a person with gray hair now, I no longer suffer much from fluctuations of mood and energy. Such ups and downs are normal for younger people and those who are transitioning to middle age, both men and women. Aging itself, in this regard, has been a gift from the gods. But just so I don't get too smug about my more stable moods as I age, the gods have also perversely robbed me of energy and good sleep (see Chapter 5, Staying Healthy). I do miss those high-energy days. But whatever your age, if you are a doctoral student working on your final assessment project, whether a monograph dissertation or a compilation of articles, you may find that your energy and (metaphorical) IQ fluctuate for any number of reasons, from natural biological ones to a (bad) decision to sleep less in order to make more time to meet dissertation deadlines.

I am guessing that some of my academic colleagues and students who have had sleep problems during dissertation writing or while working on other major writing projects resort to prescription sleep aids, which, for better or worse, I still have resisted. Alcohol, too, I understand, may initially help us sleep and soften the sharp edges of stress, but alcohol goes through one's system fairly quickly and then wakes us up. I learned early on not to drink anything after dinner—no caffeine, no alcohol. And too much of either can wreak havoc on our mental acuity the next day. Exercise is supposed to help, but I am not sure how much. Even though I walk every day, I still have nights of poor sleep. But if those of you with sleep problems can recognize patterns (such as one good night followed by one bad night or the effects of caffeine or alcohol), then you can decide wisely about how to address the problem. In all cases, it is possible to choose writing activities to suit your patterns of high- and low-IQ days. What doesn't work is taking the attitude that we should stop all writing activities until we feel better. It is, in part, accomplishing something, anything, that will help make us feel better if we are short on sleep or feeling brainless for other reasons, even if it is just proofreading a few paragraphs.

Here is a comment by Mayumi Asaba (email, September 2017) on how she tried to manage her sleep during her doctoral dissertation writing. Like other students, Mayumi sometimes felt the stress and guilt on going to bed that she had not accomplished enough on that day, rather than taking comfort in what she had accomplished:

> Someone told me that when I go to bed, I should think of all I did on that day rather than what I didn't do. I constantly feel a sense of guilt that I am not doing enough. So this advice was so helpful. I also remind myself of all I have achieved—defending a proposal on this day, finished collecting data on that day etc. When I see an overall picture, I know I am making some progress.

Clearly stress is a culprit in addition to age that exacerbates poor sleep and lowers IQ. Certainly younger scholars, including dissertation writers I have worked with, face pressures and anxieties that interfere with the clear and focused thinking needed for dissertation work. If you are one of these, you may teach full time, have family responsibilities and problems, be facing impossible deadlines for your dissertations or other major writing projects, and possibly be dealing with health issues. Such stresses can cause you to lie awake with your minds racing and hearts pounding, ensuring that there will not be a productive writing session the next day, unless somehow the adrenaline carries you through until you drop from exhaustion (see more on stress in Chapter 5). Exhaustion might at least lead to some nourishing sleep. In all these cases, it is important to identify what might be causing the low-IQ days and to find ways to work on some aspect of the dissertation in spite of them.

But if work on the dissertation is impossible, then other life requirements beckon that don't require such mental energy. Here is what Merrill Swain said about her low-IQ activities during her dissertation writing days. It looks like she wisely did not attempt to engage with dissertation writing at all on those days: "On low-IQ days, I did all the other things one has to do to live—buy groceries, take the garbage out, do the laundry, cook, etc. I engaged in what I call 'productive procrastination'!!" (email, July 1, 2018). I like the term *productive procrastination* because it focuses on the useful activities one can do on low days that we would all hate doing in the midst of a flow session of dissertation writing. Her list also includes, as she says, things we all have to do to live, unless we have servants or spouses who wait on us hand and foot.

In other words, "writing" does not always mean the high-IQ work of creating new text, processing and synthesizing readings, or imagining themes and stories that will convey our messages in coherent form in a dissertation or other major project. Writing can also refer to the dozens of routine tasks that accompany the creative tasks that we need to do to support our writing and our living. Writing could also include private and reflective writing, such as that done in journals (Casanave, 2011) as a way to work out ideas and problems that arise during the process of writing. I have urged all the doctoral students I work with to keep a dissertation journal, for example. Still, it is difficult to do this kind of reflective journal writing on low-IQ days, let alone dissertation writing. On such days, the more mechanical tasks await us. In my own case, I have never tried to assess the proportion of creative writing tasks I do to ones that are more mechanical, but I am guessing that most of us need to spend at least as much time on the routine and mechanical writing activities as on the brilliant flashes of text-producing activities. In this regard, we can embrace the low-IQ days as ones that are essential for getting the mechanical tasks done as well as for getting our laundry done and our garbage taken out.

Stories of Some High-IQ Days

High-IQ days are gifts from the gods that are given after a restful night, when stresses have been reduced, health is good, and political news is not overwhelmingly depressing. They come, too, with that feeling of "being on a roll"—when creative juices and fluent language and thinking flow easily (Csikszentmihalyi, 1996). It is on these days that ideas descend upon us while we walk, shower, doze before sleeping or waking, and even while we face the computer screen. We feel intelligent, or at least competent, if not brilliant. Words come easily, our vocabulary becomes richer, sentences fit together and paragraphs cohere. Insights happen, lights appear at the ends of tunnels, optimism pushes us forward, and our self-critical personae fade, for the time, into the background. I am guessing that we even become more fluent in our second languages on such days such that words and syntax and ideas flow nearly as smoothly as they do in our L1. On high-IQ days it seems possible to actually look ahead to finishing a high-stakes project like a monograph doctoral dissertation, collection of dissertation articles, or a book. It is on such days that real writing gets done. We can save the proofing, checking of citations and reference lists, and formatting for another day, a low-IQ day, when creative juices have temporarily disappeared. In other words, if you attend carefully to your low- and high-IQ days, you can plan activities accordingly, and so always feel a sense of accomplishment at the end of the day.

Genuinely high-IQ days might be quite rare. Many positive forces need to merge—good sleep, good health, good personal and work relationships and activities, some adrenaline, and just enough pressure to keep us from procrastinating without debilitating us with anxiety. Focus and depth and concentration help prevent distractions and interruptions, which are deadly to productive writing sessions and to the sense of flow that comes from full immersion in a creative task (Csikszentmihalyi, 1996). But paradoxically, it can be especially challenging on high-IQ days to focus on just one task at hand. On those wonderful high-IQ days it might seem as though we can do multiple tasks and do them all well and efficiently. Why not set a goal on such days of getting real writing done and also getting revising done on both a literature review chapter and a Methods chapter? Why not draft and proofread at the same time? Some people refer to this ability as multitasking, and indeed, some people seem to be able to perform multiple activities at the same time. However, the human brain cannot really multitask, even on high-IQ days, unless most of the activities have become routinized and can be performed without thinking. For instance, I can read and walk at the same time, but only if I am walking on familiar ground unmarred by rough terrain or obstacles that require me to pay attention to my footing. I can cook and talk on the phone at the same time as long as I am preparing a familiar dish. I can type and think and look out the window at the same time when I know what I want to say and because my fingers know the keyboard so well.

But we can actually concentrate on only one difficult or new activity at a time (such as either reading or writing for the dissertation). If it seems as though we are really doing more than one thing at a time, it is likely, as I mentioned in the previous paragraph, that one of the activities has become routinized, such that we can do it without thinking, or that we are moving rapidly from one task to another (Google "the impossibility of multitasking" to see what has been said about this issue, for example, and Goldhill, 2015, discussed briefly in the next chapter). In the latter case, some people, unlike me, are probably able to shift their focus from one task to another so rapidly that it seems as though they are doing multiple intellectual tasks at the same time. Such a skill has been labeled "threaded cognition" (Salvucci & Taatgen, 2008, 2011), but multiple tasks performed at the same time need to draw on different resources and channels of processing, and on a combination of new and learned resources. Salvucci and Taatgen (2008) noted in an analogy with cooking that some of the procedures in a complex activity like cooking seem like multitasking because memorized instructions have been transformed into activities that can be performed concurrently rather than needing to be performed sequentially. High-IQ energy is not required for the memorized routines. As they express it: "Threaded cognition initially relies on memorized instructions but transforms a skill to a more highly proceduralized process through learning" (p. 104). In some situations, they say, "Multitasking can seem nearly effortless (e.g., walking and talking); for other situations, it can seem extremely difficult if not impossible (e.g., reading and listening to two distinct sentences) ..." (p. 101).

However, the actual writing of new material for a document as complex and creative as a dissertation does not involve many routinized (low-IQ) processes beyond what our fingers and eyes know of the keyboard—the motor skills required for typing and proofreading. Those of you for whom typing skills have become embodied routines, done without close attention to the keyboard, can think and type at the same time if you are constructing text from familiar materials and ideas. But if you are creating new text, rather than just transferring well understood ideas to the computer screen, compiling references, or proofreading, you are doing more than combining motor skills with existing chunks of intellectual resources. You are constructing knowledge, not transmitting or transferring it. Knowledge creation like this is possible only on what I have called high-IQ days. The new knowledge has not yet become proceduralized, so you may have few of the memory chunks that can be used as a static "declarative resource" (Salvuccci & Taatgen, 2008, p. 104). Such memory chunks might be available to you later, once the doctoral dissertation is done and you are publishing further work from it.

Still, sometimes on high-IQ days, new writing and ideas and inspiration come in spurts during dissertation writing, giving you the sense that the drafting is not as difficult as you feared or as it is on the low days. I envy writers who are blessed with many such spurts and who can switch quickly and with concentration from one bit of new writing to another. All of us need to find a way to take advantage of such high points and not postpone the writing until later. By the time "later" comes, the ideas and particular wording may have evaporated. And spurts of inspiration may be short and descend upon you at inconvenient times. If you don't already have strategies for recording ideas that come to you at odd moments of day or night, you can keep some kind of recording tools close by—apps, including small paper and pencil notebooks, laptops, or book-style computers that live strapped to your body. Ideally of course, high-IQ writing sessions will happen in settings that are conducive to writing, at moments that are free of distractions and interruptions, and not in the middle of the night or during teaching sessions or meetings.

In other words, dissertation writing—meaning the construction of new text rather than the mechanical work that is also part of the process—gets done best on high-IQ days when focus on new and difficult tasks can happen in uninterrupted and relatively lengthy spurts of concentration. We are multitasking only in the sense that our brains, eyes, and fingers are working at the same time on the same project. We are not performing two new tasks at the same time (Salvuccci & Taatgen, 2008, p. 107), but our minds are working quickly and creatively. It is impossible to prescribe ideal times and places for this kind of uninterrupted and creative dissertation writing, because writers differ so greatly in their preferences. These range from writing in total isolation to writing in the company of like-minded friends and colleagues, and from total silence to the din of coffee shops and of music feeding into the brain through headphones. Successful dissertation writers learn about and understand their own preferences and needs for what they can accomplish on high- and low-IQ days, and follow what they know about themselves. You can become one of these successful dissertation writers.

Somewhere in Between

In the end, all the creative and intellectually challenging tasks will eventually get done by a tenacious dissertation writer, whether you pick away at many small subtasks in a writing session or concentrate only on one thing, and whether writing of different kinds happens on high- or low-IQ days. I don't know how to write in very small spurts, and so must use my high-IQ days for periods of uninterrupted and focused writing on a single task. I know when to stop, or when to switch to a different task, because the creative juices dry up or because it's time to cook and eat something (brains need food). All of us can also use the low-IQ days, as I said, for mechanical dissertation tasks and for laundry.

It might be that I have exaggerated the distinction between high- and low-IQ days, and that most writing days experienced by dissertation writers are characterized by more neutral periods of effort. The distinction between what happens on high and low days probably gets highlighted because it is the extremes of emotions and energy that we usually remember, not the routine days where no doubt many productive writing episodes happen. But I also hope to remind myself and others that it is on the extreme days that all of us need to be especially attentive to applying appropriate strategies in order to make the most of very different energies and motivations that we all experience. It makes no sense to end a low-IQ day in total frustration because we were not able to construct even a single good, let alone brilliant, paragraph. Likewise, it probably makes no sense to end a high-IQ day feeling that we have accomplished no more than correcting typos in a reference list. A waste of good brain power? Maybe, but still a necessary part of writing. How can you adjust your dissertation writing activities to the energies and motivation of particular days? It might be a strategic idea to make a list of all the different high- and low-IQ activities you can do on appropriate days so that you can go directly to the list that suits your mental powers for the day. A list is especially useful on low-IQ days, days that can be accompanied by indecisiveness, guilt, and frustration. Importantly, in the midst of dissertation writing, especially for those of you who are on strict deadlines, all activities matter because they all need to get done. What is counter-productive is for you to dither just because you are not sure how to deal with your ups and downs.

SUMMARY OF MAIN POINTS

1. It is normal for dissertation writers to experience high and low days of mental energy and motivation.
2. Dissertation writers benefit from understanding why they might feel very productive on one day and "brainless" on another.
3. Strategies can be employed to take advantage of both high and low days in order to accomplish different kinds of dissertation-related activities, from highly creative tasks to mechanical ones.

SUGGESTIONS FOR DISCUSSION AND REFLECTION

1. In your dissertation writing and other doctoral work, do your mental energy and creativity fluctuate or are they relatively stable? Do you believe these fluctuations are under your control or subject to uncontrollable influences?
2. Have you ever experienced a "flow" state during dissertation writing? Describe this, and try to explain why this happened.

3. How do you explain how your own brain seems to work to accomplish what you need to get done? What similarities or differences do you notice with classmates or colleagues who are also writing dissertations? Talk to them about this if you have not done so before.
4. What strategies do you employ during your dissertation writing to accommodate differences in your mental and physical energy on different days? What changes (realistic ones, please!) would you like to pursue in your writing strategies?

Chapter 7

Loneliness and Isolation

"After completion of predissertation requirements, the candidate finds himself adrift, with accustomed educational support systems withdrawn to a degree unprecedented in American education at any level."

—David Sternberg, 1981, p. 26

"The thing that surprised me most about PhD study is how powerful the sense of being alone can be. [...] It's not until they are gone that you realise how important **classmates** *are. [...] We shouldn't dismiss these feelings of loneliness and alienation in ourselves as 'just whining' because they can have real consequences."*

Inger Mewburn, The loneliness of the long distance thesis writer, *Thesis Whisperer* blog, October 26, 2010

Students who have finished course work or do not have regular meetings with study groups during dissertation writing are likely to experience the loneliness and isolation of the long-distance dissertation writer (cf. David Sternberg's chapter "The Loneliness of the Long-Distance Writer" in his 1981 book on surviving a doctoral dissertation and Inger Mewburn's blog entry from 2010, cited in the epigraph, "The loneliness of the long distance thesis writer"). It helps if dissertation writers are simultaneously working in a job where they have contact with others (such as teaching), but the actual dissertation writing time is generally very solitary. Feelings of social isolation during graduate work have been linked to high rates of attrition (Ali & Kohun, 2006, 2007), so isolation is a matter needing attention by both doctoral students and faculty. This chapter describes the benefits for dissertation writers of in-person writing groups, writing partners, or peers with whom to share experiences and possibly drafts, and in the absence of such connections, of seeking even one or two online connections. Solitary writing can also be embraced as a "friend," a convenient way to focus totally on oneself and one's project.

Writing Alone or with Others

When I had finished course work, dissertation proposal, data collection, and preliminary analysis for my doctoral program, I quit my part time teaching job on campus, left my rented room, and came home to write. I could not afford to be out of a job for too long, so felt some pressure to finish without delays. I was glad to be home, but I am not sure that I was prepared for the isolation of full-time writing in the privacy of my own home, away from classmates, students, and advisers. At that time, we did not have social media that could routinely connect us by video—technology that can cut through the sharp edges of isolation. I am also not sure what difference it might have made had I stayed near campus or had such technology, because wherever I was, I would have had to sit in a chair for many hours a day, alone, writing. I did not know how to write a book-length research report, and even if I had been surrounded by my doctoral classmates, we were all in the same boat, in new and sometimes rough waters, not yet recognizing the precious luxury of this time in our lives.

But at least I was living at home, and for part of the last year was teaching an MA TESOL course and so escaped total isolation. I was lucky. International students everywhere suffer doubly because they are far from home country and family. In his study in the UK, Hopwood (2010) found that for the doctoral students he was working with, "Living at a distance from partners, children or parents presented challenges, prompting negotiations and leading students to find means to deal with physical separation" (p. 111). Living with a partner or family presents other problems, because family members need to find a way to adjust to prolonged absences from the dissertation writer (emotional, physical) even if the writer resides in the same place. The writer in all cases needs to set up a dissertation space where uninterrupted writing can happen (Hopwood, 2010; Mewburn, 2019b; Sternberg, 1981).

In another study of students from Hong Kong pursuing doctoral degrees in Australia, the researchers found that the "international students spoke about desperately missing home, their country, and their families and friends" (Fung, Southcott, & Siu, 2017, p. 187). It is astonishing that any doctoral students in such situations manage to finish their dissertations. I was isolated during my dissertation writing, but for the couple of hours a week of teaching I did, but not the way my international classmates were. Perhaps without the isolation and the solitude, the writing might not have gotten done, or might not have gotten done as fast as it did in the case of students living far from home. For all of us, the isolation helped prevent too many interruptions and distractions that could easily have broken the rhythms of writing and the single-minded concentration needed to complete the project (see more on distractions in Chapter 8). Still, periodic social connections with other dissertation writers can help keep dissertation writers accountable and, I must add, sane.

When I was in the midst of dissertation writing, I did not consider how writing groups, writing partners, and writing retreats might have helped me (Aitchison, 2009; Guerin, 2014; Kamler & Thomson, 2008; Paltridge, 2016). Would they have helped cut the sharpness of the solitude and provided emotional and intellectual support, or would they have interrupted my need to focus only on my own writing? Would it have made a difference if such a group were organized by a faculty member or by students themselves? Where would I have found such a writing group, when all the people in my cohort had scattered, and were facing the same pressures to get drafts done and revised by a deadline? Perhaps if my circumstances had been different, and if I had still been living on or near campus, I would have been able to stay connected the way Robert Kohls described during his dissertation writing:

> Doing a PhD can be isolating, but you can combat that isolation by actively staying connected to colleagues and friends. While working on my PhD, I met with friends to talk about our research, shared drafts to be critiqued, wrote together, and presented research together. That time together helped to keep us focused, productive, and connected. Socializing is an important part of completing a PhD as is exercising and eating right. I knew that after I graduated, life wouldn't get any easier. Learning to stay connected and to juggle a healthy lifestyle during your PhD is the dress rehearsal for the hectic life as a faculty member afterwards. (Robert Kohls, email, October 18, 2018)

This description from Robert sounds ideal, but because I was living far from campus, the year of my dissertation writing was one of the most solitary and self-absorbed periods of my adult life, as it was for those classmates who had also left the university area or maybe even returned to their home countries to finish their writing. As isolating as it was, there were certain pleasures in this focus on the self during the writing period. Given this understandable self-absorption, we were not in a good mental and emotional space to devote concentrated attention to each other, to learn about each other's writing problems, or to help each other through difficult writing challenges and blocks. I wonder if this solitary dissertation writing would have been different had my situation been different—had I been in closer proximity to other warm-body dissertation writers. I'll never know, but if you are a connected and social dissertation writer who can still manage to remain focused on your own dissertation writing, you are fortunate indeed.

In my case, given my geographical distance from the university in my last year of writing, and perhaps because of my rather solitary nature, I felt as though I could survive only by focusing on my own work, so as not to lose my train of thought or break the flow of my writing. I was never good at regular socializing, nor—more important—at the mythical multitasking that some talented people seem to be able to do, as I described in the previous chapter (Salvucci & Taatgen, 2008, 2011). The need that I had, and that some others probably have, for solitude and single-task focus to get serious writing done is supported by research, some of which notes that multitasking is scientifically impossible (Goldhill, 2015). Some of this research includes the view that multitasking in academic contexts actually involves "divided attention and non-sequential task switching for ill-defined tasks as they are performed in learning situations" and the view that "human information processing is insufficient for attending to multiple input streams and for performing simultaneous tasks" (Junco & Cotten, 2012, pp. 505-506). In other words, people who claim to multitask are actually quickly switching focus from one task to another. I don't know how dissertation writers can complete their projects working in this way, but perhaps some writers have talents that I lack. Note that I do not consider reading and walking at the same time or touch-typing and looking out the window at the same time to be cases of multitasking in the context of academic performance. Such tasks do not require equal attention in the way that trying to work on multiple chapters at the same time does, or that revising a chapter while texting a friend does, or that trying to write one's own drafts while attending to the writing needs of classmates or students does.

Here is an example. In one unfortunate event, in the midst of my solitary doctoral dissertation writing, still vivid in my mind many years later, a classmate who had been part of a small group of women who tried to support each other during course work and proposal writing called me at home long distance, asking for help on a difficult part of her own dissertation writing. It was mid-morning and I was in the midst of a solitary concentrated writing session, and her call jolted me out of my train of thought. Rather than asking me if it was a good time to talk, she began reciting her problem, expecting me to listen at that moment and to offer suggestions. But I could not switch gears fast enough to focus on what she was saying, so deep was I into my own solitary dissertation writing. And I was distressed that she had not asked if the timing of her call was good for me, and so with regret cut her off rather abruptly. Our friendship suffered as a result, and I proceeded for the remainder of my dissertation writing on my own and she sought help elsewhere. I was left wondering if any dissertation writers have time, energy, or motivation to focus on anyone but themselves during those crucial months of intensive writing. I think some do, but I was not one of them.

However, doctoral dissertation writing groups have been used in ways that I was not aware of when I was writing and can help cut the isolation (Aitchison, 2009; Aitchison & Guerin, 2014; Paltridge, 2016; Roulston, Teitelbaum, Chang, & Butchart, 2016.) Some of the literature on doctoral dissertation writing suggests that social support can be a lifeline for students. Although there were a few research groups in my doctoral program in which a small group of students worked with a faculty member on one of the faculty member's projects, to my knowledge our program did not have faculty who set up or encouraged student writing groups or study groups devoted exclusively to students' sharing their work, including attending to their emotional needs (Wellington, 2010). Moreover, the small cohort that I belonged to was scattered geographically once our course work was done, making it difficult for us to meet regularly. We did not talk about, or hear talk about, small group mentoring, either in person or from the yet-to-be invented online forum (Kumar & Johnson, 2017). Some of us occasionally shared drafts with each other, but rarely with our advisers, who we guessed wanted more complete work, so meetings with advisers happened infrequently. Lave and Wenger's (1991) work on situated and participatory learning had not yet been published, so writing was still treated as an individual and solitary endeavor for the most part, at least in my experiences in the program. Moreover, busy advisers and faculty committee members were not interested in the real-life encumbrances experienced by adult, even middle-aged, dissertation writers (Jazvac-Martek, Chen, & McAlpine, 2011) and probably students themselves were reluctant to share personal obstacles to their writing. If students did not produce drafts for advisers to look at, meetings did not happen. Having said all this, I must note that if another of my cohort members had written this chapter, the tale might be very different. I do not know how unique my experiences were. Readers will need to compare their own experiences.

In the remainder of this chapter, I will elaborate on some issues about loneliness and isolation, and also about writing support groups, as discussed in some of the literature and blogs on doctoral dissertation writing and as provided in anecdotes by a few brave students and colleagues who have been willing to share their stories with me. Remedies, such as they are, can also be found through internet searches, in blogs and other resources, some of which I will comment on briefly. However, it is my understanding that despite what some of the literature and anecdotes say, dissertation writing ultimately remains a solitary activity at the drafting stages. In the section that follows, I present some counter-views that challenge my beliefs.

The Paradoxically Social and Isolating Activity of Writing

Although there is a stereotype of writing as a solitary activity (picture Annie Dillard [1989] sitting alone writing in her cabin in the woods with the windows covered), writing has long been recognized as a fundamentally social and cultural activity (Berkenkotter, Huckin, & Ackerman, 1991; Bruffee, 1983; Nystrand, 1989; Prior, 1998). For instance, in composition, rhetoric, and English for academic purposes in North America, "there has been a discernible shift away from notions of language and writing as a discrete skill or stand-alone attribute, to a recognition that language and writing is a complex, context-specific social and cultural practice" (Aitchison, 2009, p. 906; Bazerman, 2004; Prior, 2006). This practice is situated within what have been variously called discourse communities, communities of practice, disciplinary communities, research communities, institutional discourses, socially motivated genres, and activity systems, among other terms for groups of like-minded people in academia who support each other in person and increasingly online (see https://thesiswhisperer.com). Even if we are not envisioning an in-person community as such, disciplinary writing includes at the very least a professor and a student (Fujioka, 2014) and people who know (of) each other through publications. The older cognitive process view of the individual writer planning and drafting and revising (Flower & Hayes, 1981) in relative isolation has been replaced by more socially-oriented perspectives (Aitchison, 2009; Ivanič, 1998).

The socially motivated nature of doctoral dissertation writing cannot be denied (Kamler & Thomson, 2014). People undertake doctoral work for social, not just intellectual, purposes, usually to become or remain a member of an academic community. Not only purposes, but also processes and contexts of dissertation writing are deeply social. Academic communities consisting of departments within universities are social institutions, populated by people of all kinds—faculty, administrators, staff, students—though we may rarely see some of these people in person. Even an online presence is still a social connection, such as in distance education and online advising. At some level, we can also say that students are interacting with others, namely with authors, through their reading. Moreover, a doctoral dissertation, itself shaped by others, is written primarily to be read by others, whether by a handful of committee members or by future scholars interested in a research topic. A doctoral program and dissertation, in other words, cannot be completed or have influence in the academic world if writers work in total isolation. A dissertation is a social document, produced in sociohistorical and sociocultural conditions (Prior, 2006).

Why, then, does doctoral work at the dissertation writing stage seem so isolating and solitary? Perhaps, in spite of the complex social and interactive work that goes into the preparation of the writing of this high-stakes document, it is because the actual chore of constructing lines of words on paper or screen (Casanave & Sosa, 2008) is a labor-intensive activity that only one person can do in a single-authored document like a monograph dissertation or dissertation article. Though not talking about dissertation writing, Annie Dillard begins her book *The Writing Life* with this observation: "When you write, you lay out a line of words. The line of words is a miner's pick, a woodcarver's gouge, a surgeon's probe. You wield it, and it digs a path you follow. Soon you find yourself deep in new territory: Is it a dead end, or have you located the real subject? You will know tomorrow, or this time next year" (Dillard, 1989, p. 3).

Dillard continued by describing the box canyon at the end of the path, the need to throw words and lines away, the need to "demolish the work"—often what you feel are the best parts—and start over: "The part you must jettison is not only the best-written part; it is also, oddly, that part which was to have been the very point" (p. 4). In Chapter 9 on Revising, I discuss further the central activity in the writing process of not just constructing sentences but also of throwing them away, an act that can actually be greatly aided by trusted readers who are not so attached to the words.

Not all of us are such tortured perfectionist writers as Annie Dillard, but we can feel the solitary aspects of the activities and choices that will eventually evolve into a dissertation and maybe later a book. Unless someone else—a supervisor, faculty member, fellow dissertation writer, or professional editor—actually writes and rewrites for the dissertation writer, the bulk of the work is solitary even as it is socially situated. This work rolls out day after day in lines of words that may or may not be read and helped along by others and that may or may not find their way into the finished product.

Isolation in an Internet Era

It is odd to think that dissertation writers might be more isolated in an age of electronic connectivity than before social media devices and small portable computers made it possible to write anytime anywhere and share everything with everyone instantaneously. Yes, it is true that our electronic connections with others have mushroomed, and even the dinosaurs in the academic world cannot imagine how they survived without these instantaneous connections with people and information from around the world. From this perspective, it is possible to argue that isolation is not even a phenomenon worth mentioning. None of us is truly isolated. Connections are a click away.

However, these are not warm-body connections. Isolation in this electronically connected world can still pervade a writer's life, a world that may even contribute to it. In the first place, in spite of assertions over many years that writing is a social act (Bruffee, 1983), the act of writing itself is so fundamentally solitary that internet connections, to say nothing of in-person contacts, with friends, colleagues, and faculty, can easily be interpreted as interruptions in the writing process. In my own work on this book and on other projects, I am struck with how ubiquitous internet interruptions are, even if I try to ignore them. Each time an email arrives, a notice flashes across my screen and adds to the number of unanswered messages in my email inbox (most of them trash, but they still have to be sorted). I do not have the will power to turn off this function. If I respond to all the messages, or any of them, even if just to delete unwanted spam, my train of thought is disrupted and my ideas lose focus and efficiency. Yes, I am connected to others, but in order to get any focused work done, I must pretend to ignore them. At some level I am glad these connections are there and that I too can reach out across the world to others in a keystroke, but they still constitute interruptions in what would otherwise be focused writing sessions (see Chapter 8, including the comment by John Hedgcock about turning off his internet connection altogether during writing sessions). And they are no substitute for warm-body connections if you truly want to connect with others.

Internet connections are addictive, however, and the important ones happen so much faster and easier than if you try to arrange meetings with fellow writers over coffee, impossible if a writing partner lives far away. It is also difficult to ignore internet connections even in the midst of focused dissertation writing or writing on other projects. But don't those of you in the midst of writing have to find strength and strategies to ignore internet interruptions and temptations as one way to help you focus your attention on the writing to be done? In other words, at some point during dissertation writing, isolation of various kinds needs to be embraced as a friend to writers. And although internet and social media addicts will no doubt disagree with me, I think internet connections and social media somehow need to be put aside during focused dissertation writing sessions.

Of course, isolation cannot be total. When you have something to share, or something to discuss before writing, or when you feel blocked, internet or in-person connections with others feed into the dissertation project and help move it along. But I wonder if dissertation writers consider whether people they are reaching out to for help on a moment's notice might themselves be immersed in a state of solitary focused writing and see the request for help as an interruption, as happened with me and a cohort member, described earlier in this chapter. I don't know how easy or difficult it is for individual dissertation writers do this kind of perspective-taking, switching from a focus on self to a focus on others, but it was difficult for me. Perhaps my experiences would have differed had I been part of a dissertation writing group.

Dissertation Writing Groups, (Boot) Camps, and Focus Groups

Even though the lines of words in a doctoral dissertation are constructed for the most part by solitary brains and hands, the context for writing can be as social as circumstances and personalities permit, in the form of writing groups and focus groups, boot camps, and writing partnerships. As I mentioned earlier in this chapter, I did not participate in such groups when I was writing my dissertation. However, the academic writing I have done since moving back to California from a decade-plus of post-PhD teaching in Japan has happened mostly in a school library, where at any moment I can witness other people reading and writing, silently processing thoughts or churning out words as part of their own academic endeavors. I don't know these people, but they are as fully engaged with lines of words as I am. Yes, we are all solitary readers and writers, but we form a community of scholars by virtue of the fact that we are all seated in the same quiet space working on something. (I exclude the young man sitting across from me as I write this, a fat book open on his lap, but his face in his smart phone.) But the people working in this library are not organized as a writing group.

I have, however, occasionally organized weekend writing retreats at the school with which I am loosely affiliated. I find that even though I sit in the same chair in the library and look out the same window as on other days when no writing retreat participants are present, on writing retreat days, I feel a sense of accountability to myself and to other writing group participants to get something done on the project I have committed to. In the presence of other writers, I make special efforts to avoid distractions to the extent possible, and to share with the participants my perceived successes and failures for the day. Even if the participants are few, we all benefit from mutual encouragement and support, especially when the work is slow and the energy for it is low. We are still solitary writers, but we are not alone.

But writing retreats happen infrequently, so I try to maintain this writing-group sense of accountability on all the other days I sit in the library, even when no writing group participants are present. I am not sure why I cannot enforce such concentration on myself at home, but sitting in a quiet room full of books and other people who are (mostly) working seems to help with focus and to fulfill a need for both solitude and connection.

Dissertation boot camps offer writers a way to situate themselves periodically in a social group that is designed specifically to support dissertation writers. Boot camps now seem quite common at many universities and are championed by some L2 writing experts, as are other kinds of dissertation support groups (Crusan, personal communication; Russell-Pinson & Harris, 2019; Vandrick, personal communication). They offer a shared space and structured schedule for dissertation writers over a period of several intensive days or regularly such as once a week or once a month during a school term, and may even include snacks and organized discussion. The dissertation boot camps sponsored by universities follow certain policies and regulations, all designed to combat students' isolation and provide encouragement, accountability, and social connection to writers. Claremont Graduate University describes dissertation boot camps this way on their website:

> "Dissertation Boot Camp is a writing retreat for graduate students who must balance their dissertation writing with the demands and responsibilities of home and work. Boot Camp offers students a quiet space to write without distractions or interruptions. The CWR provides a light breakfast, lunch, snacks, and individual spaces for focused writing. [...] Boot Camp develops writers' ability to set effective goals and to track their own writing processes. In addition to providing a dedicated space for a weekend of writing, Boot Camp helps students find sustainable writing habits that move their work forward. In addition, we become a community of writers committed to completing our dissertations on schedule, supporting and cheering each other on, and sharing strategies and experiences to help each other navigate the dissertation process with our sanity intact!" (https://mycampus.cgu.edu/web/writing-rhetoric/home/dissertation-boot-camp) (accessed November 16, 2018).

An internet search turns up sites at many universities that could be used as models for graduate students and faculty at universities that do not host their own writing days. Look up, for example, to see what is offered by Stanford, Princeton, University of North Carolina-Chapel Hill, Claremont Graduate University, UCLA, and Northern Illinois University.

Dissertation boot camps might not exist on your campus, or convene regularly enough for some dissertation writers. Writers themselves could organize these, but such organizing takes time and energy away from the your own writing. Still, it might be worth trying. Informal dissertation writing groups of other kinds not only can help you with strategies and encouragement for moving your writing forward, but also can provide you with needed emotional support during the potentially very stressful and isolated writing time. In such groups, you can openly share your blocks, fears, and doubts with each other, which left unattended can derail you and possibly lead to your withdrawing from the doctoral program. The emotional side of dissertation writing can overwhelm writers with "stress, fear, isolation and anxiety" (Wellington, 2010, p. 146). In isolation from others, you are left on your own to confront the emotionally taxing experience of figuring out whether what you are writing is on track and adequate, and then of waiting for and receiving feedback from a faculty adviser. Those of you who participate in writing groups can support each other through these difficult times during writing, even if you don't provide each other with specific feedback on drafts. Writing groups can also help you figure out how to respond to changes that have been requested on a draft that took you weeks or months to prepare, help you lower your resistance to requests for changes, and help you understand that such requests are not personal attacks. Groups can also be used as outlets for you to vent emotions and frustrations in ways that could not be done in the presence of a faculty adviser or family member or in the solitary setting of an office.

I discuss attitudes and emotions further in Chapter 9 in the context of revising, but for now will just sum up by saying that interactions with fellow dissertation writers in writing groups or with writing partners can help you survive the isolation, emotional ups and downs, and insecurities during the potentially lonely period of drafting and redrafting. Connections with other writers, in person or online and with or without the specific help that peer readers can provide, can cut through the isolation and give you a sense of shared understanding of what other writers are experiencing, and can reinforce commitment to a shared purpose and long-term goals. For those of you with a more solitary nature or in more isolated circumstances, the uninterrupted if potentially lonely time can be embraced as a friend that can contribute to progress on writing. After all, the sooner the dissertation is finished, the sooner one's social and family life can resume.

SUMMARY OF MAIN POINTS

1. Dissertation writing is an inherently solitary experience during actual writing time.
2. Dissertation writers differ in their needs for solitude and connection during dissertation writing.
3. Study groups of various kinds as well as writing partners and dissertation boot camps can provide dissertation writers with much needed connection and emotional and intellectual support.
4. Internet and social media connections can paradoxically contribute to both a writer's isolation and connections with others.

SUGGESTIONS FOR DISCUSSION AND REFLECTION

1. What are your own experiences of feeling either isolated or connected during your dissertation writing time?
2. How much solitude and how much connection do you need to be the most productive on your dissertation writing? How do your needs for solitude and connection differ according to the dissertation writing stage or task?
3. To what extent do you need or participate in connections with others online or in person during dissertation writing? What is your preference?
4. Do you have any experience with dissertation boot camps or writing retreats, or know if your university hosts them? If so, discuss these experiences with other dissertation writers. If not, try to learn about them to determine if they might suit your needs during dissertation writing.

Chapter 8

Distractions and Interruptions

"Even if you lock yourself in a room to focus on your thesis writing, distractions in your mind will always be there. Thoughts pop into your head about your career, the bills, your family, and that thing you forgot to pick up from the store (for the 3rd time!)"

—Dora Farkas, January 20, 2019

When dissertation writing gets especially difficult, often in the middle or towards the end of long months of drafting when deadlines loom, it is easy to get distracted, to procrastinate, and to prioritize more pleasant activities and postpone the unpleasant. In Chapter 4, I discussed some of the reasons why writers get stuck and procrastinate (perfectionism, writer's block...) and possibly find themselves stalled to the point of giving up. In this chapter I discuss other reasons why writers might get sidetracked in the midst of dissertation writing without consciously deciding to set dissertation work aside, and suggest that following some writing rituals and habits—if writers are not already doing this—

can help keep them on track. Some distractions and interruptions are a normal part of many dissertation writers' lives and not easily avoided, such as family life or other relationships, or working at labor-intensive jobs that can take over one's life (teaching and administration). Both of these distractions—relationships and work—of necessity, should take priority, but sometimes don't, with the result that families and work, rather than dissertation writing, are neglected. Many writers are also familiar with other more banal but soothing distractions such as organizing office files, watching TV, feeding an addiction to texting and other social media, cleaning house, doing laundry, attending to other household chores, and eating chocolate. Some of these distractions are required to keep our lives running in some semblance of order. Others? Maybe not.

Those of you who, in the midst of your writing, find yourselves distracted to the point where you are not making any progress need to look closely at possible reasons why. I hope that such introspection has a happy ending, such as completion of the dissertation, but in some cases, such reflection could lead to escape and withdrawal from a program, even once dissertation writing is well underway. Let me be honest and say that for some dissertation writers, withdrawal from a program might actually be the happy ending, if reasons for continuing are not compelling and if misery hangs over your life like a suffocating black cloud. In other words, you might be distracted because it really is time to move on to something else. But in many cases, if you are a distracted writer, you will benefit from looking in the mirror, seeing the circles under your eyes, and acknowledging that it is indeed time to buckle down and finish. You will also benefit from recognizing the joys and pleasures of this precious time of your lives, during which self-absorption can actually be framed as a virtue and a gift to be nurtured.

Nevertheless, it can be especially tempting for those of you who cannot devote yourselves full time to your writing to distract yourselves with other academic work (teaching, conference preparation, manuscript reviewing, grading papers, administrative tasks), with the argument that all such work is necessary for an academic career. Yes, this work is necessary, but it can easily be used as an escape from dissertation work and in many cases can be justified as taking priority over writing. Other time-consuming work is closely related to the dissertation: Reading, note-making, discussion with others, and thinking are essential for getting a dissertation written, but can easily continue without a clear end point. In all cases, you will be inclined toward activities that are more enjoyable or more immediately pressing than actual dissertation writing, and may find yourselves slipping away from your drafting.

My own work on this book project is a good example. Even though I am not consumed by classroom preparation and in-person teaching duties (now part of my more youthful past), I have gone weeks, or even months, without working on this book, because other work has more pressing deadlines, such as doctoral student advising or manuscript reviewing or conference preparations and travel. How easy it is to put other work first, to say nothing of giving in to life's daily interruptions! And then, as I contemplate diving back into actual writing, I can persuasively convince myself that more reading awaits me that I must accomplish before I can write knowledgeably. Yet many sources I am familiar with on thesis and dissertation writing, indeed all academic writing, apply to my own writing on this book draft and all say the same thing—try to do something every day, or at least every week, and don't pretend that you need to read more if you have already done plenty. Although I am not always a good role model in this regard, it is essential for you to manage interruptions, write regularly enough so the project doesn't "go cold," and devise strategies for staying on track if you hope to complete the work. Specific strategies and writing rituals and habits are individual matters, but they need to be identified and pursued. (Note the confidence with which I make this assertion; I hope it does not ring hollow, given my own struggles!)

Productive and Unproductive Distractions

I began notes for this chapter thinking that all distractions from dissertation writing are unproductive. However, on further contemplation, I think I was mistaken. Let me begin with an obvious reason why some distractions can be ultimately productive for dissertation writing.

Brains need rest. Down time. Rejuvenation. Expansion. Distractions can potentially provide some of these benefits, as long as they do not totally replace writing time or take over our lives. A person who plays ping-pong for distraction from intense mental work will get exercise, time away from language-focused brain work, and at least one social connection. However, if that person begins dreaming about winning the next game, decides to try some competitive play, or looks ahead only to the next game rather than to the next chapter, trouble brews. More dangerous than ping-pong and other physical activities are academic or dissertation-related activities that seem pertinent to the project, but that actually distract from and interrupt the immediate dissertation writing task of the day. For example, those of you who are also teaching writing may find that you are always driven to spend more and more time helping students learn to write rather than doing writing yourselves. Teaching writing can be a highly labor-intensive activity, particularly for teachers who commit to helping students both draft and revise. Of course, if the topic of your dissertation concerns writing and the teaching of writing, the time-consuming work of teaching can feed into and inspire the dissertation, leading you to believe you need still more data even if you are in the midst of writing (all so close at hand, so why not?). But teaching can also dangerously replace writing time. After all, the actual classroom contact hours spent teaching might be minimal compared to preparation time, consulting with students, and marking papers.

In other words, if you are a dissertation writer who also teaches and has become consumed with the work of teaching, your own writing can fall by the wayside. Students that we teach come first; they cannot wait, and if you are paid to teach, you must fulfill your teaching duties. You may also find that teaching can be a nourishing, addictive escape, justified in more ways than I can count. How easy it is to be convinced that teaching must be prioritized because it is required for our livelihoods, because it helps others, and because it might also feed into a dissertation topic. The priority is equally compelling if you love teaching (not all dissertation writers do)—a most productive distraction indeed. In short, distractions such as teaching can be productive, providing mental engagement and rejuvenation, inspiration for writing, and a livelihood in the form of a paycheck, as long as they don't consume your life. Regular writing time must somehow be carved into your schedule, where "regular" means more than once a month or even more than once a week, as my own adviser warned me. If you are one of those fortunate graduate students who is being supported by grants and fellowships for several years and does not have to work, you are the envy of many, but distractions still lurk. Here are a few more thoughts.

Family, Relationship, and Work Distractions

I begin this section with distractions stemming from personal relationships and work because these cannot easily be postponed, set aside, or controlled. Whatever personal relationships a dissertation writer has, a *place* and a *space* must be set aside in your life for work to get done (McMullan, 2018). Obstacles to place and space abound. If you are a dissertation writer who is a mother or father and if your spouse is not available to help much at home, you cannot make children disappear during dissertation writing unless the dear young ones are pawned off to in-laws, day care, or boarding school, or unless a spouse becomes more available for childcare (Mewburn, 2019b). Likewise, a wife or husband or partner who needs attention cannot disappear for a year or more in order to allow you undistracted time and space to write without severe consequences for the relationship (and yes, divorces and break-ups happen). Moreover, cultural expectations for gendered family duties may cause more stress for some students than for others. Even if you are happily single, you might choose to care for a pet that requires almost as much attention as a human family member, possibly more. You cannot walk away from your dog or cat, even for a day or two, without shipping it out to a kennel or arranging for a neighbor to care for it. Pets are part of your family, and though you may talk to them at length, they will never understand your absence, or fulfill your vain hope that they occasionally cook their own dinners. (Good luck teaching your dog how to do this.) Unlike your pets, your few precious relatives, friends, and colleagues usually will understand what you are going through, even if they are unhappy at your long absences from their immediate presence. And at least you don't need to groom and walk them or clean their litter boxes daily.

Still, a life that is purged of all such warm-body distractions (though I guess it is hardly appropriate to demean them by calling them distractions) might contribute to your focus and single-mindedness. Theoretically, a solitary life during dissertation writing can help you concentrate just on writing and revising. But such purging could result in a life empty of relationships that need nourishing if they are to endure once the dissertation writing is completed. Dissertation writers themselves need nourishing with warm-body distractions. As I indicated in the previous paragraph, these include relationships with pets, for those so inclined. We don't often learn about these warm-body distractions and impositions in the life of a dissertation writer or in the books on dissertation writing, even in ones as personal and engaging as Meloy's (1994, 2002). Perhaps Inger Mewburn (2019b) comes close in her personal reflections on "becoming an academic"—a book revised from her Thesis Whisperer blog posts that she has written for many years (https://thesiswhisperer.com). We learn stories from her of Mr. Thesis Whisperer, and of Thesis Whisperer Jr., and how somehow she managed to get through her dissertation writing and early academic career without major damage to her relationships with her loved ones.

We do occasionally hear about routine academic distractions that get in the way of focused work on dissertations and on other major projects. Jazvac-Martek, Chen, and McAlpine (2011) collected "progress logs" from doctoral students in faculties of Education at two universities in Canada to learn about the daily realities of their doctoral work, including many activities in addition to thesis and dissertation writing that could be considered distractions. These included attending meetings with students and supervisors, writing conference papers, applying for funding, preparing for comprehensive exams, reading literature, and conversing with peers. In general, the doctoral students in this study were well networked in their academic circles, not doctoral hermits, so all these extra activities were normal and expected, if time-consuming, and generally occurred before students were deep into their actual writing.

Many of the students' dissertation-related activities in the Jazvac-Martek et al. study involved interactions with other people at the university or at conferences, as is the case for working faculty, but the students in this study interacted less often with family and friends. Family and friends helped in the sense that they provided space and emotional support for the dissertation writers (p. 24) yet at some level they did not always understand the writer's prolonged absences. Many of the writers in this study experienced difficulties that dissertation writers will be familiar with: exhaustion, intellectual dead ends and blocks, loss of motivation, financial worries, constant time pressure, a sense of isolation, and the feeling of being neglected by supervisors. Moreover, PhD students in the social sciences tend to work in isolation rather than with teams of researchers, as is more often the case in the sciences (Levecque et al., 2017). All of these difficulties stemming from realities in writers' personal and professional lives represent potential distractions from the focused work of dissertation writing. As Sue Starfield explained in an email to me about the benefits of the thesis-writing boot camps at her university, "One of the things the students who come to the writing boot camps say is that the boot camp helps them avoid distraction" (email, August 8, 2019) because they are not writing in isolation. They are accountable to each other in ways they are not if they work alone.

But even with a supportive group, trying to balance personal and professional goals is always tricky, especially for women (Kurtz-Costes, Helmke, & Ülkü-Steiner, 2006; McMullan, 2018; Mewburn, 2019b). One result is that mental health problems are more common among women PhD students than among men (Levecque et al., 2017). Not surprisingly, difficulties and sacrifices experienced by women are especially painful, given that dissertation writing might be perceived by them and loved ones as a distraction from family life rather than the other way around. Strong traditions in some cultures and families make it especially difficult for women to put themselves first as they pursue higher education degrees, and the "emotional labor" of maintaining family duties and writing a dissertation can be tricky to manage (Aitchison & Mowbray, 2013). Mewburn's (2019b) positive experiences as an academic with a young child are probably rather rare—her non-academic husband fully supported her, filling in with household duties as needed. Others are not so fortunate. One of my doctoral students whose daughter fell ill halted all dissertation work for many weeks (both her daughter and her dissertation survived in good health, as did her marriage). Several other of my female students tried to take care of elderly parents, write their dissertations, and teach at the same time. Other writers, male and female, reported feelings of growing distant from their family and friends, with the attendant consequences of ill health and depression. What I earlier called "heart work" (Casanave, 2014) cannot be neglected without repercussions. In short, family obligations inevitably interrupt a dissertation writer's concentration and drafting time, but also provide needed stability, support, and connections for both men and women. This strong emotional base will help you persist and combat tendencies to procrastinate (Russell-Pinson & Jafarian, 2020). Family and friends are essential distractions during this stressful writing time (Hopwood, 2010) as long as they are not used as excuses for not writing.

Managing Distractions

Distracted doctoral dissertation writers risk ending up ABD (All But Dissertation). I do not recommend putting "ABD" after your name on your business card if you aren't able to finish your writing, even though getting this far represents a significant achievement. Some time ago, it even took on its own status as a semi-legitimate moniker (Sternberg, 1981, pp. 2–3), but for those who understand the initials, it signifies an unfinished journey. It makes more sense to figure out what is distracting you from finishing and to learn to manage the emotional and professional conflicts and interruptions that might be getting in the way of your finishing. Managing conflicts and distractions at the dissertation writing stage is particularly challenging, however, because the structured graduate work and data collection that came before have been completed, and you are on your own to get your writing done. As one author phrased it: "Often, until the dissertation, students have functioned in a rather structured environment, with clear sequences of courses, classes at particular times, term papers due and exams on specific dates, etc. Suddenly, none of these apply, and students must structure tasks and time for themselves" (Blum, 2010, p. 77). If you are mid-career dissertation writers, you might have little difficulty structuring your dissertation writing time and managing your distractions simply because as working adults, you have already had many years of practice in organizing your complex lives. At the same time, you probably lead lives that are full of real-life distractions that younger writers have yet to encounter, such as those associated with family and career (Mewburn, 2019b).

Whatever the sources of distractions and interruptions, you either find ways to manage them and to finish your writing, or to give in to them, and so postpone finishing or even withdraw from your program. Because managing distractions is such an individual matter, I can't prescribe specific corrective strategies, beyond two basic ones: First, become aware of what distracts you and when distractions and interruptions are most likely to happen. Second, establish some productive writing habits and follow some writing rituals if you are not already doing so. I end this chapter with a few anecdotes about habits and rituals that some colleagues described to me, all of which seem designed to help keep writers on track and so prevent distractions and manage interruptions.

Writing Habits and Rituals

It may come naturally to some people to set up and follow productive writing habits and rituals (terms I am using interchangeably, although linguistic purists will complain: Rituals are intentional; habits are automatic). Whatever we call them, repeated purposeful actions can help you manage distractions and continue working on a dissertation or other major writing projects even in the midst of a busy complex life. Such people tend to thrive on predictable schedules, orderly computer (and/or paper) files, and regular eating and sleeping habits. Regular writing habits can help you produce text on a steady basis and reduce or control anxieties you may experience. Writers for whom regular writing comes easily might be able on your own to analyze your writing habits and rituals and establish and adjust them as needed. Other writers might benefit from consulting published work on strategies for dissertation writing and supervising (Bolker, 1998; Marias, 2016, Paltridge & Starfield, 2019), participating in dissertation writing support groups or retreats (Paltridge, 2016; Roulston, Teitelbaum, Chang, & Butchart, 2016), or by taking advantage of writing professionals on your university campuses (Russell-Pinson & Harris, 2019).

In the midst of dissertation writing, you will probably benefit from the order and accountability such groups and counseling provide. It is embarrassing to confess to your writing group or supervisor that you are easily plagued by distractions and that yet another day has gone by without a word being written, although you will probably discover that you are in good company. Whether you are in a group or consulting with a writing partner or professional, dissertation writers of all kinds, not just those who are easily distracted, will benefit from being asked specific questions by fellow writers and mentors about your writing habits and rituals (Russell-Pinson & Jafarian, 2020) and learning how other writers organize their time and manage distractions and interruptions. I don't mean to imply that writing habits and rituals need to be slavishly and compulsively followed. Indeed, it is likely that productive habits and rituals include some unpredictability amidst the structure and regularity.

Writing Ritual Anecdotes

Writing rituals can occur at any stage of writing, from planning to drafting to revising. Here is a list of what John Hedgcock refers to as a "pre-writing" ritual, and a comment on a reward he gives himself for a writing session that goes well. Many of us will relate to rituals like this, ones we somehow need to follow in order to begin and then continue writing each day:

> - I always turn my radio on b/c I need background sound on (silence tortures me—instant recipe for utter unproductivity).
> - I set an app called Freedom that shuts the internet tubes for the time frame that I select. This cheap, effective internet-blocking software prevents incoming email messages, websurfing, the temptation to go down a rabbit hole searching for a source online, etc.
> - I literally clear my desk of everything and anything that isn't directly related to what I'm writing (only articles, books, and notes are allowed). This ritual helps me clear my mind.
> - Similarly, I dispense with necessary but tedious (and potentially distracting) tasks that require my attention *before* concentrating on a writing session (e.g., pay bills, check email, grade, etc.).
> - When I arrive at a benchmark (e.g., number of pages read or drafted, two or three hours devoted to a project, finishing up a section or chapter, etc.), I reward myself somehow and/or take a pause (afternoon tea, cat-break, check the mail, exercise, iron .... anything **other than** thinking hard). (John Hedgcock, email, July 12, 2019; emphasis in original)

And here is another anecdote that resonated with me from Kathi Bailey—writing rituals she followed that responded to daily weather patterns during the two years that she was writing and revising her dissertation. Kathi had just moved to the Monterey Peninsula having been offered a job to run the new TESOL Master's program at the Monterey (now Middlebury) Institute of

International Studies. Like me, she took a job before she had completed the writing of her dissertation, and was faced with writing when she could in between work duties. In her case, she crammed a lot of writing and revising into two summers that spilled over into a couple of semesters. I had warned her about moving to Pacific Grove here on the Monterey Peninsula, a lovely town, but often dripping with fog in the summers—gloomy, and not usually conducive to cheerful and energetic bursts of writing. But gloomy weather can keep dissertation writers glued to their chairs when otherwise they would be outdoors playing. Here is what Kathi said about that time, and about the rituals she followed:

> One thing I can tell you about the ritual aspect—and it has to do with living in Pacific Grove. You may not recall but I remember you told me before I arrived here that 1981 was one of the foggiest summers you could remember. (Someone told me—don't know if it was you—that people in Pacific Grove don't tan—they rust.) During the two summers, I'd write in my home office in the morning while it was foggy. Then about 11 AM when the fog lifted, I'd go out and work in my little vegetable garden and read whatever I needed to read for updating the lit review. Then about 2 PM when the fog rolled back in, I'd go back to the home office and start typing and revising again. The fog kept me on schedule. (Kathi Bailey, email, June 28, 2019)

Writing rituals like these work in part because they build distractions and interruptions into the ritual itself. The distraction, if it can be called that, becomes a sort of reward for work accomplished. Perhaps these rewards should not even be labelled "distractions." In addition to functioning like a reward, they provide you with moments of respite and refreshment, needed to help prevent you from burning out. The trick is to distinguish such needed moments of respite from desires to escape. If you are not feeling nourished at regular moments in the actual dissertation writing process, you will naturally use distractions to escape rather than to refresh your energy and intellect.

Another colleague, Stephanie Vandrick, wrote me about the writing habits she follows in her very busy life (full time work, committee duties, family) in order to accomplish various writing projects such as conference papers, chapter contributions, and book drafts. She listed some routinized activities that are useful to her, and told me that she hopes they will be useful to others:

1. I try to set aside time for writing, and put it in my calendar.
2. I really like to write with others, in scheduled writing days or writing retreats.
3. I prefer to write in a "third place," not my home or office, when possible—e.g., a conference room, or a library.
4. If I am working on several projects, and don't have an immediate deadline, I work on whatever "draws" me that day.
5. Sometimes I work on two or more projects during the same writing session, consecutively.
6. I always re-read what I wrote the time before, and then begin that day's work.
7. At the end of a writing session, I send the newest version of my writing to myself via email, and print a copy.

8. After writing, I text a long-time writing friend about when and how long I wrote. (Stephanie Vandrick, email, July 15, 2019)

What is notable about this list of writing habits is first, that Stephanie schedules regular writing sessions, often through her university, and puts them on a calendar; second, that she needs a place to write outside her home; third, that she can manage to work on several projects in a single day (unlike me); and fourth, after a writing session, she shares her accomplishments with a friend. Although not everyone will be able to manage multiple writing projects, most of us can benefit from regular writing sessions in a familiar and comfortable place and from support from others and from one's academic department. The group support, as well as a single writing partner (the "long-time writing friend" she mentions), provide her with a sense of accountability that seems to be one of the central benefits of maintaining a schedule and contact with other writers. If begun in graduate school, these writing habits and rituals, all designed to manage distractions and keep you on track, can support you throughout an entire career.

And finally, here is a blurb from Deborah Crusan about the very sensible rituals she followed while writing her dissertation:

> I would first have to re-organize the folders I was working with that contained data—student essays, rubrics with scores on them. Then I would sit to write. I wrote every day for about 4 hours for about 2 months. I would get a can of Diet Coke, put on some music, and write. One thing that helped me was re-reading what I had written the day before and editing, revising, reworking, until I could move on to new

> writing. The old writing got me into the new writing by helping ideas to fire in my brain. (Deborah Crusan, email, June 24, 2019)

As is evident from all four of these anecdotes about writing habits and rituals, productive writers structure their time so as to work regular writing sessions into their daily lives and to manage the inevitable intrusions of email and other social media. Such regularity and predictability help you resist the killer distractions partly by building some smaller needed distractions and inevitable interruptions into your schedules. Productive dissertation writers also find ways to get a jump-start on their daily writing, usually by re-reading what they had done in their last writing session. And they are likely to have favorite places and times to write, either solo or with others, for their regular writing sessions. As I and my doctoral classmates were advised long ago, advice that still stands, do not wait till vacations to do your writing. Make regular writing a part of your life, and find ways to manage your distractions. By following some regular writing patterns that enable real, even if slow, progress on your writing, you might actually learn to love the writing, and manage the distractions. But if you can't learn to love the writing, at least you can learn to do it.

SUMMARY OF MAIN POINTS

1. Distractions and interruptions that divert dissertation writers' attention away from writing are normal, particularly for students who are working and who have families.
2. It is essential for dissertation writers to prioritize their activities carefully during the dissertation writing period so that distractions do not take over their lives.

3. Some distractions, such as job searches, family issues, and the need for breaks, cannot be avoided.
4. Monitoring distractions and the extent to which dissertation writers have control over them can help writers develop strategies for staying focused.
5. Establishing productive writing habits and rituals can help dissertation writers manage distractions and interruptions and stay on track.

SUGGESTIONS FOR DISCUSSION AND REFLECTION

1. How easily are you distracted from dissertation work? What kinds of things tend to distract you from dissertation writing and interrupt your writing sessions?
2. How necessary or inevitable do you believe various kinds of distractions and interruptions are during the time you are trying to write your dissertation?
3. How easy or difficult is it for you to focus fully on your dissertation writing without being distracted or interrupted? If you are easily distracted, what advice can you give yourself and others like you?
4. What kinds of writing habits or rituals do you follow that help you manage productive writing sessions and resist distractions? What suggestions do you have for others who might be easily distracted and would benefit from some adjustments to their writing habits?
5. How do you manage the inevitable interruptions that life imposes on dissertation writers?

Chapter 9

Revising

"... [R]evising and editing happen to everyone, and are not emergency procedures undertaken only in cases of scandalously unprofessional incompetence."

—Howard Becker, 1986, p. 46

"In all, there are as many perfect dissertations out there as unicorns. The 'accepted but with revisions' outcome ... is the practical best-case scenario."

—David D. Perlmutter, 2015

From one perspective, this chapter presumes that writers have drafted enough of their dissertations to be able to consider some of the inevitable revising that must take place. Such revising work can be especially demanding toward the end of dissertation writing, particularly if students are no longer in love with their dissertation projects or are simply too fatigued to imagine surviving the tedious work of revising the entire draft. Doctoral students who are in this unenviable position need to recommit at the revising stage to finishing.

But revising happens at all stages of dissertation writing, not just at the end. Therefore, this chapter covers revising activities that accompany and follow from the initial drafting of a dissertation project on to its completion, whether of a sentence, paragraph, chapter, entire monograph-style dissertation, or (as in some programs) articles for publication. These revising activities might be self-initiated, but they also often occur in response to critical commentary, which can come from many different sources and take many forms, some more benign than others. The revising activities that are prompted by self and others include (re)reading, cutting, pasting, rephrasing, expanding, rearranging, backing up, cutting corners, tossing, keeping and saving, and proofing—activities that cannot be taught prescriptively, because they vary too much among writers. In this chapter I don't discuss work such as proofreading—more of a technical activity that comes at the end of spurts of writing and then in serious ways when drafts are complete. Instead, I focus on larger changes and attitudes that happen during writing itself. The point will not be on how to revise, but how to think and feel about revising activities, including on work that you might not love anymore because it is no longer new and challenging.

Prescriptions for Revising? Not Likely

Here is an example of exactly what I will <u>not</u> be saying about revising in this chapter, from a book on "writing the winning thesis or dissertation" (note the use of the "should" word and the imperatives in the prescriptions):

> You should also revise as you write. Most good writers revise as they write, following a procedure that goes something like this:

> Write a paragraph.
> Stop and read what was just written.
> Revise that paragraph.
> Write another paragraph and start the cycle all over again. (Glatthorn & Joyner, 2005, pp. 140–141)

Not all resources on dissertation writing offer advice as prescriptive as this. Moreover, I cannot think of a single time when I wrote and revised in this way. If you can write and revise this way, you have my blessing. I also found it odd that some resources on dissertation writing that I looked at did not even have an entry in their indexes for revising, even though it is basic to all high-stakes writing (Cooley & Lewkowicz, 2003; Glatthorn & Joyner, 2005; Meloy, 1994, 2002; Paltridge & Starfield, 2007, 2019). Even Becker's classic book on thesis writing (1986, 2007, 2020) has very little on revising, and Sternberg's 1981 book *How to Complete and Survive a Doctoral Dissertation* has just a couple of pages. Serious and sustained revising might be addressed only if the goal is to help writers turn their dissertations into books (Mulholland, 2011).

In reality, specific revising strategies evolve individually with each dissertation writer and so cannot be taught prescriptively. But in all cases, regardless of specific techniques, revising involves many kinds of alterations in which you discard things you have written as well as change text in large and small ways. You may be anxious about changing or throwing away what you have already drafted (This is part of me! I worked for days and weeks on this! Don't make me throw it away!) (see my comments on Annie Dillard's writing in Chapter 4). You may therefore feel resistant to or threatened by criticism and by suggestions to revise or rewrite from supervisors, from others, and even from your own self-critiques. It is also possible that as a long-suffering dissertation writer, you resist revising because you are just tired of your project, and tired in general, by the time you need to do final revisions. Resistance to revising can thus come from fatigue. This chapter will help you accept the normality of these responses and the normality as well of the work of rewriting and revising any major high-stakes project, both during and after drafting.

In fact, revising can be tremendously gratifying in that it involves polishing and dare I say "beautifying" the language. But beware of the other side of revising—the compulsion to continue revising ad infinitum, particularly for those of you with perfectionist tendencies (see Chapter 4) or low confidence, until you are forced to stop by external pressures (see Chapter 10). Such an approach to revising will be extra burdensome, beyond what it needs to be. Better to attend to meticulous revising when you are working on the publications that follow after you graduate. Do what you need to do at the dissertation writing stage to complete a passing final assessment. That's all you need at this point.

The Myth of the One-Draft Dissertation

It is probably the dream of every doctoral dissertation writer to do a one-draft dissertation or series of articles that will magically be accepted by a supervisor and a defense committee or by journal gatekeepers without needing to be revised again. So much work has already gone into the drafting of the major opus that it is difficult to imagine mustering the energy, motivation, and time to do anything more than minor touch up and proofreading once the initial draft has been produced and in particular after it has been defended. But of course revising inevitably happens after a defense in addition to ongoing revising during writing, even if published advice on dissertation writing does not always emphasize this (Paltridge, 2002). Still, at the end of many months or years of dissertation writing, it is almost inconceivable before a dissertation defense to imagine the additional revising work that needs to follow within a relatively short period of time, to say nothing of possible future revisions of the opus into articles and a book. If you have successfully defended your draft, you no doubt would prefer to sleep for a month or go on an extended luxury cruise. The fatigue and loss of mental energy that come after a defense are real, particularly if you have lost interest in and enthusiasm for the work or if you feel that the dissertation still needs more substantive work. Don't give up.

However, before the revising that happens after the defense comes the ongoing revising that you do during the actual writing, before a defense takes place. Such revising might be inspired by your own critical eye. This critical eye never goes away, and if you feel compelled to continue reading to update your knowledge of pertinent literature (called "readitis" by Mewburn, 2019b), your critical eye could get even more critical. For instance, gatekeepers who review your work love to inform you of further reading that could or should be done. But continued reading, in spite of all its benefits, can expose all the gaps yet to be filled and so can lead to painful choices if there is no time remaining in the doctoral program to fill them. These gaps can be filled in future work, post dissertation, but at the time, it might feel like this future work will never happen.

A dissertation writer's critical eye is essential, but the revising that counts most heavily before and after a dissertation defense comes in response to feedback on your chapter drafts from an adviser and possibly from one or more committee members and peers. For both L1 and L2 writers, some of this feedback will be linguistic, at the sentence and lexical levels, and relatively easy to address in revisions. Some dissertation writers even pay someone to do this tedious work. The more challenging revising tasks are those at rhetorical and content levels, where you might be asked to clarify meaning, re-think and flesh out arguments, re-organize sentences and paragraphs more "logically," consult the work of someone else who has said the same or opposite thing, or link a literature review chapter to a discussion chapter more effectively. So much for the mythical single-draft dissertation.

You might not get specific suggestions from others on how to do these more challenging revising tasks—on how to clarify meaning or present an argument more logically or make links with literature. Supervisors and faculty might assume that both L1 and L2 students at the doctoral level should already know how to do these kinds of revising tasks. On the other hand, if you are required to submit your work for publication as part of the doctoral process, or complete a "dissertation by publication," then revising will also happen in response to (sometimes harsh) critical reviews from outsiders such as journal reviewers and editors. The best critical reviews from faculty, peers, or outside reviewers will offer specific suggestions for revision, which at the time could seem overwhelming in their detail and in their sometimes contradictory advice. At least if you receive detailed feedback, you are not being neglected or rejected, and you will have a sense of what to do. But even if not all feedback is consistent, maximally constructive, or writer-friendly, revising needs to be done.

Revising happens at so many different stages of writing a doctoral dissertation that it is easy to view dissertation writing as primarily the activity of revising. At one level, this observation is so commonplace and so expected that it is quite unremarkable. I cannot imagine that either students or faculty have ever experienced writing any important text and getting it right in the first draft, but I suppose this is possible. Even if there is only one extant draft, and no evidence of revision on that draft, it is likely that revising happened word by word, both on screen or paper as well as in the writer's head. If changes that happen along the way are not saved, and if multiple drafts are not collected and numbered, the final text will reveal no evidence of the extent to which the author revised. I sometimes number my drafts, which often go through five or more versions (my record is 20), and other times I work on and change just a single draft, as I am tending to do for this chapter. Each time I go back to work on it, I reread what I have already drafted, tinker with it (making small or even large revisions), and then move on to further drafting and revising. The older incarnations have disappeared, but they existed at one time, and often much was changed on them.

This is not to say that occasional spurts of brilliance and "flow" (Csikszentmihalyi, 1996) might not result in passages that need little revising. This does sometimes happen, but I don't know how common the flow experience is, either in my own writing or in the dissertation writing of L1 and L2 doctoral students I have worked with. It is a wonderful feeling, if rare, to have words tumble out that still make sense the next day, and then the day after that. I think it also might be the case that little revising happens when time runs out, and we are not able to do much more than proofread what we have perhaps hastily drafted. But ordinarily, as I am doing right now with the few paragraphs in this section, words are added, deleted, rearranged, and re-thought as I write. And once I leave these paragraphs to move on to others, these same paragraphs await my rereading, rethinking, and revision for another day (see more anecdotes on writing rituals and habits in Chapter 8). Not many of these paragraphs will see the light of day unrevised, even if I am lucky enough to produce a few passages under "flow" conditions.

The Emotions of Revising

The very act of writing a long and complex doctoral dissertation is fraught with emotions from start to finish (see Sternberg's 1981 extensive discussion of emotional problems of dissertation writers and supervisors), to say nothing of the emotions of revising. Emotions at the thought and process of revising dissertation drafts vary greatly among individuals, but can run high, in both positive and negative directions. Revising always involves change, letting go, accepting input from others, and in general, making large and small adjustments to text that has already been drafted, sometimes with great difficulty. Many writers also identify closely and personally with what they have written, so changes to drafts can feel like more than textual changes. They can feel like changes to and even "assaults" on oneself, feeding a writer's fears and sense of inadequacy. Self-doubt can undermine success for both L1 and L2 doctoral students, particularly those L2 students who are not fully proficient in English (Ingleton & Cadman, 2002). Revising thus requires confidence, an emotion that is considered "a key to success" in doctoral work (Cotterall, 2013, p. 98), but that can be rare in dissertation writers.

The kinds and strength of emotions during revising also depend on the sources of feedback to you and the extent to which you can exercise agency in your learning experiences (Hopwood, 2010) and in your decisions about what and how to revise. Dissertation writers can be their own sources of critical feedback, of course, as you go through the relatively solitary process of writing, reviewing, and revising and re-writing without input from others. Sometimes you are your own harshest critic, such that emotions of inadequacy and self-blame surface at various points during revising. Awaiting and responding to feedback from others, however, leads to different emotions, because the critiques are coming from outside the self, most often from more powerful, if not harsher, critics than oneself. One scholar remarked that "one of the most emotional aspects of the process of writing a thesis or an article is the business of awaiting, anticipating, fearing and then receiving feedback on writing..." (Wellington, 2010, p. 137).

Emotions on receiving feedback and on facing the sometimes tedious task of revising can also be very positive and motivating when the overall message from an evaluator, whether faculty or peer, is encouraging. Imagine the different emotional responses that you might have to a message that says "This is a great draft; here are some things you need to do to make it ready for a defense," and one that says "This draft is not ready and still needs a lot of work before you can think of defending it." Although the draft might be the same, and the messages are essentially the same (the draft is not yet ready to defend), the wording of the first message will motivate you to forge ahead with energy and enthusiasm. The second message might undermine your confidence or spark an angry reaction from you. Additionally, feedback expressed in a less personal or more critical tone can alter your fundamental commitment to the work as a result of the mixed or negative emotions a negative tone produces. Here is what one of my former doctoral students said about reviews she got on a manuscript that she submitted during her dissertation writing to a domestic journal: "I received feedback that I felt was a bit rude (most probably there was no intention at all on the other end to be rude but the feedback still seemed not thoughtful and informed enough); it took me a long time to even try to write my response" (Natasha Hashimoto, email, August 22, 2019).

It is normal that emotional investment is high in doctoral work, particularly in the midst of dissertation drafting and revising (Mewburn, 2019b), and for some of you, emotional responses can influence whether you forge ahead with energy and motivation or reluctantly, if at all. You, not just your texts, will be judged on this work, after all. As Caffarella and Barnett (2000, p. 49) noted in their study of doctoral student writers, "graduate students, and most professionals, are judged on what they write. With the stakes so high regarding their writing ability, it is not surprising that graduate students are so emotionally invested in how their work is critiqued." (Note that the authors say "how" their work is critiqued, not "that" their work is critiqued.) The point is that the emotions of confidence and motivation can be built or undermined by the type and style of critique, with "personalized, face-to-face feedback [...] and the iterative or ongoing nature of feedback" most responsible for building confidence (Caffarella & Barnett, 2000, p. 47). With such personalized feedback, revising might not become fun, but it will at least be considered normal as one of the most important ways to improve the dissertation draft. Moreover, you will know that those who provide personalized feedback are invested in helping you improve your drafts. Uncomfortable emotions might not disappear, but they will not undermine your confidence and commitment.

Who Revises? (Or: Who Owns My Writing?)

One of the first times I wondered about the question of ownership in the revising process was when I read Paul Prior's 1995 article on response, revision, and disciplinary enculturation. In that article, Prior closely analyzed the responses made by a professor to six drafts of a conference paper written by "Moira," a sociology doctoral student. The responses mainly took the form of edits by the professor to the student's text rather than general commentary or suggestions, allowing Prior to count words that had been added, deleted, and rearranged, mainly by the professor. In essence, the professor rewrote many sentences of Moira's work and Moira accepted most of the changes, causing Prior to ask whose meanings and voice were being expressed in the revised text. In the case of this doctoral student, we cannot say that she revised the paper. The revising and rewriting were done jointly, in the sense that the professor rewrote and Moira accepted the changes. As Prior observed, "The student's conference paper displayed the student's accurate, indeed almost total, compliance with the professor's proposed revisions" (Prior, 1995, p. 289). Although Prior talked about "negotiated meanings," there was little evidence in this revising process as reported by him of a balanced negotiation of voices and textual changes.

By the time I read Prior's 1995 article, I had already completed my PhD and coincidentally written my own article on writing activities in a sociology doctoral program that I had studied as part of my dissertation work (Casanave, 1990, 1995). I wanted to document the "local interactions" that students and faculty went through as students completed their written work and learned the jargon of the field. Students were hardly able to resist the input of powerful faculty, and a few students who continued to feel out of place writing and speaking in a way that felt inauthentic eventually left the program. I wondered then how these students were able to learn to write and revise their work in accordance with the conventions and language of sociology, and indeed how I was learning to write and revise according to the conventions in my own doctoral program, beyond copying styles from our readings. Was it even possible to write and revise without giving up ownership of one's work? Or is it impossible for novice scholars to own their own work at the early stages of their academic careers?

On relooking at Prior's and my older work, and more recently at Li's studies of Chinese novice scientists writing for publication (2015, 2019), I have to travel back in time to remember what kinds of responses I got to my own dissertation drafts and what I did with those responses. As was the case with Moira, I received comments written by hand on print drafts, not directly in a computer file, and recall being a bit surprised at some penciled rewrites by my adviser of phrases and sentences. Like Moira, I accepted most of these changes. In other cases, I was asked to read something that I had not included, or to reinterpret my comments on a reading I had written about. I recall that my ignorance of the literature, in particular of which scholars were best known in an area and which ones were allies or antagonists, made it very difficult for me to write and revise in a way that resulted in an authoritative voice that I could own (Thompson, 2012).

In a nutshell, during my doctoral dissertation work I did not know enough to be able to revise well. My revisions, based as they were on the input of a faculty member and on imitative phrasings from my readings, pretended authority. They were performances that were not yet embodied (Casanave, 2019). They took on the tone of a disciplinary expert, but the experts were the faculty members who were guiding me and the authors that I was reading and from whom I was borrowing words. Of course in some sense I owned my revisions. But my writing and revising experiences from those days, in conjunction with my reading on the topic, convinced me that indeed it is true that there is probably no such thing as a solitary writer who is the sole owner of a text. Revising in particular is done in response to direct or indirect input from others, not just to the self as critical reader, such that ownership is always partly handed over to others.

However, heavy-handed involvement of a supervisor in the writing of novice scholars has been reported by Li (2015, 2019), in both doctoral work and novice scientists' early publication efforts. In the case of doctoral supervisors in China helping students with English language theses, dissertations, and publications, pressure on both supervisors and students is fierce, given requirements for students to publish papers in recognized English language journals in order to graduate (Li, 2015). Rather than teach novice scholars how to write, the supervisors that Li studied wrote or rewrote sections of students' papers in the revising process, and the novice scholars generally simply accepted the changes by incorporating them into subsequent drafts. In a paper co-authored with a supervisor, particularly in the sciences where co-authoring is the norm, such involvement might be expected, but I thought less so in doctoral dissertation revising.

I don't know how common this type of joint "revising" is at the doctoral level, with such deep involvement of a professor or supervisor and general lack of guidance provided to students on how to revise high-stakes work like a dissertation. Such involvement was documented some time ago not only by Prior (1995) but also by Blakeslee (1997). She described the case of a novice scientist writing for publication and his supervisor's involvement in (re)writing. As was the case in Prior's and Li's work, the novice scholar in Blakeslee's study compliantly accepted his supervisor's revisions. Perhaps it is just easier for supervisors to rewrite students' drafts than to try to make explicit what is needed for students to revise on their own. This might be the case particularly if the writing involves a publication required for students to graduate from a doctoral program and if the supervisor's name is included as co-author. As Li found, dissertation supervisors do not consider themselves to be writing teachers, and they do not have the expertise needed to teach students how to write or revise. Bitchener and Basturkmen (2006, p. 6) explained the same phenomenon this way: "[S]upervisors themselves tend to have tacit rather than explicit knowledge of the features of the thesis in their own disciplines." In other words, they can do the writing and revising for themselves and others, but possibly not be able to teach it, even though they may have much needed disciplinary expertise (Gube, Getenet, Satariyan, & Muhammad, 2017). In other words, organizing and displaying knowledge is not the same as having it. Whoever does this revising work, it will involve sometimes painful changes and compromises that dissertation writers need to make under high-stakes power-infused conditions.

Conclusion: Coming to Love the Dissertation Garbage Bin

Revising, in part, involves throwing things away in addition to rewriting. Some people find it much easier than I do to throw things away, whether from a computer file, or from a table top, a desk top, or a closet. (Not pretty places, my closets.) I can only imagine the sense of freedom that such people have on keeping computer files, desks, and closets tidy and organized and cleared of all files but for those that writers are working on or clothes that they are wearing. Inger Mewburn (2019b) described how she discovered Marie Kondo's organizing strategies (https://konmari.com) and managed to empty out both her closets and her computer files of all but the essentials. How liberating it must feel to throw out unused drafts, or even parts of drafts, in the process of revising, rather than clinging to a "just-in-case-I-might-need-this" attitude, the way I do with some 20-year-old clothes I no longer wear and with some drafts of written work. When I worked so hard to construct this chapter or paper draft, even writing in my L1, discarding it seems cruel. I can only imagine if I had constructed a "throw-away" draft in my L2—how much harder it would be to revise, rewrite, or discard it because it was so much harder to write.

But "letting go" in the process of revising does not need to mean permanently disposing of previously constructed text, if you balk at doing this. With rethinking and revising, temporarily discarded words might actually come to life and find a place in a future article or book. Of course, I can't think of many times when I actually did need something that I had moved into the metaphorical garbage bin, but I find it soothing to think that if I chose to do so, I could resurrect old drafts and notes from folders buried somewhere in my computer. Drafts do not end up in my real garbage bin until I am truly ready to let go of them. Unless I make a mistake. It was a great shock to my system when a couple of years ago I lost my main working folder by emptying the trash on my computer where I had mistakenly dragged this working folder (my fault). For some important work in that folder, I had no backup (also my stupid mistake). A "garbage bin" folder or updated backup folder and external thumb or hard drive, or even specialized recovery software, would have prevented the weeks of mental and emotional self-flagellation that followed.

Nevertheless, as I have indicated throughout this chapter, one essential component of revising is the act of changing or removing some of what you have already written, or maybe even removing all of it and starting over—painful amputations. The image of throwing early work into a garbage bin is perhaps a bit too dramatic, but I use the image to make a point. Some of what dissertation writers and other academic writers initially draft will inevitably not be used, possibly even for future work. Work that is not used might actually be quite good, but not a good fit for the dissertation project. Other work, on the other hand, might be perfectly awful, whether writers recognize this at the time or not. Peer readers are useful in this regard, and can help both novice and experienced writers know whether, when, and where to revise and what to put in the trash. In the midst of writing, it can be difficult for any of us to evaluate our own work and to decide what to keep and what to toss. Hence, the usefulness of a metaphorical electronic garbage bin that can hold deleted material until you are truly ready to let go of it and move it to the real trash. Moreover, in a recoverable garbage bin might be gems-in-the-making, seen from another perspective, another day, another set of eyes.

And revising can feel liberating and pleasurable. A former doctoral student wrote me that "I especially like doing stylistic and grammatical revisions! That makes me feel like I am learning (or reviewing) something that will be useful frequently in the future" (Natasha Hashimoto, PhD candidate, email, August 21, 2019). And Matt, whom I introduced in the Preface, a very competent L1 writer who likes revising, told me, "For me, [revising] really involves reaching a kind of 'mind-shift' and learning to let go of the hard-won 'golden prose' (usually 'false gold') and to find ways to manage the associated stress and disappointment" (Matt Prior, email, October 3, 2018). The outcome always improves.

I end this chapter by pointing out the obvious—first, that revising is impossible if there are no drafts to revise, and second, that all good academic writing results from revising. Perhaps keeping all drafts until a project is finished is not the best answer for everyone. It works for me sometimes and not others. If archiving (hoarding?) all drafts does not work for you, then some other system needs to be in place for having easy access to any materials that might be profitably revised for the dissertation or other major project. If we call this a "garbage bin," then we must be sure the garbage bin is not emptied until the contents truly are ready to be trashed rather than resurrected and revised.

Finally, just as it is possible to learn to love writing, or at the very least to learn to get it done, it is also possible to learn to embrace the challenges of revising. As Matt told me about his revising activities: "If I'm rewarded with a meaningful view [from the mountain] and a sense of accomplishment, I don't really mind the skinned knee, bug bites, cold wind, and the many hours it took me to get to the top" (Matt Prior, email, October 3, 2018).

SUMMARY OF MAIN POINTS

1. Revising is an inevitable part of dissertation writing and other professional academic writing later.
2. There are no fixed prescriptions for how to revise, in spite of what some dissertation writing guides might suggest.
3. One-draft writing is rare.
4. Revising is an emotional process because it involves changing or throwing away "part of oneself."
5. Questions of ownership arise when the work of dissertation writers is heavily influenced by others, such as supervisors.

SUGGESTIONS FOR DISCUSSION AND REFLECTION

1. How do you feel about revising your academic writing, including your dissertation drafts? If revising is difficult for you, why do you think this is so?
2. What guidelines have you read or been given about how to revise your in-process dissertation?
3. What kinds of influences have others, such as supervisors or peers, had on your revising?
4. What processes do you go through when you revise? Do you find it easy or difficult to accept the suggestions of others on your dissertation writing, including suggestions to throw out parts of what you have written?
5. Do you keep all your dissertation drafts and drafts of other major writing? Why or why not?

Chapter 10

Time to Stop

"Defining the end is not easy, as we are never, in an absolute sense, quite there."

—Judith M. Meloy, 1994, p. 79

This short concluding dialogue portrays a dissertation writer's tendency to continue writing and revising in spite of looming deadlines. The dialogue is fictional, but I think represents the feelings and experiences of dissertation writers as they near the end of their project. The sense that the huge dissertation project is not yet finished haunts many doctoral students as their deadlines near, and can cause last minute waves of panic, sleepless nights, and flight reactions. Yet every writer must stop at some point, even if you have been granted an extension. Planning a post-dissertation defense party with friends and family can help see you through to the end and help you consider what to do next. Can the dissertation be crafted into one or more articles, books, or presentations? Can it be a jumping off point for further research on the topic? Or is it truly finished because its author, you, are ready to leave it behind and move on? If you feel it is truly finished or that it is truly time to stop, I suggest keeping your books, articles, and data somewhere safe for a while rather than having a huge bonfire and marshmallow roast. You never know when your inquiry and all that is associated with it might beckon you once again.

A: (biting nails; looking under-slept; massaging carpal-tunnel syndrome wrists) I think I need another extension. I just can't finish what I have to do by this final deadline.
B: You have to stop.

A: I can't stop before the dissertation is finished, can I?
B: It will never be truly finished. You just have to stop.

A: Never be finished? What? But if it's not finished, I can't turn it in. Or defend. Or graduate!
B: It will never be finished in the way you are imagining. There will always be something more to do on it.

A: Right! That's why I need another extension!
B: No, that's why you have to stop.

A: But I just found three more really important and recent sources, a book and two articles, that I have to add, including one by my adviser. And I have to read them first, and then find a way to integrate them into the lit review, and maybe adjust my research design to show I know this work, and then adjust the Discussion chapter to match the updated lit review, and then …
B: You have to stop.

A: I mean, if I don't include these recent sources and adjust my perspective a bit, my dissertation will be outdated even before I graduate!
B: That's normal. That's why you have to stop now, so that you can move on.

A: What will my adviser and my committee say if I don't, at the very least, include these recent sources?

B: They'll remember their own dissertation experiences, including the inevitability that there will always be sources more recent than the ones you have included, no matter how many times you update. You'll never finish your reading, so you just have to stop reading.

A: I am sure that I will embarrass myself if I don't know the most recent work that has been done on my topic. I can't go public with an incomplete dissertation.

B: It will never be complete. There will always be more to do. You have to stop.

A: Even if I can make myself stop reading, I really need to go back and tweak my analysis and then adjust my interpretations. I just did not know enough when I was doing this draft for the defense.

B: No, you need to stop now, and move on.

A: But how can I move on with this flawed and incomplete document?

B: I know I sound like a broken record, but it will always feel flawed and incomplete to you, even if you spend another three months tinkering with it.

A: But at the very least I need to revise and polish the language some more. After all, I am not an expert writer by any means. Academic writing has always felt like pulling teeth, like surgery without an anesthetic, like slow torture with a torture device that looks like a computer keyboard, like abuse by the Dissertation Ogre, like....

B: Stop, please. You are bringing up too many memories for me. Just know from someone looking back on it now, you have to stop.

A: Are you saying I should just close my eyes and turn in what I have and say a few prayers?

B: Well, it's not quite that simple. Did you proofread carefully?

A: Yes, and I am doing that one more time. A colleague is helping, in trade for my walking his dog for the next two years. And I might even pay a professional proofreader as a last step.

B: Expensive. You can probably do a better job yourself, especially if the professional proofreader does not know your field and topic and specialized terminology. But if you need someone to check for small things, that might be a good idea. Just do whatever you can to make sure there are no typos, grammar problems, or formatting problems. That will just look sloppy, but it wouldn't be the end of the world for your committee members to catch a few typos. After all, they have to have something to do, right? So once you are finished proofreading, once you have made the document look pretty, you can stop.

A: I don't know. Maybe I should do one more member-check with the participants to make sure they don't have a problem with how I have represented them.

B: Didn't you do that already?

A: Well, yes, but it couldn't hurt to do it one more time.

B: But it's time to stop.

A: What if I get something wrong?

B: What if you do? You won't die. And what would "getting something wrong" mean in your case? What will happen? Will you not graduate because you interpreted something one way when it could have been interpreted another way? You have to get your facts right, of course, but your interpretations are yours alone.

A: But someone will see that I might have made a mistake.

B: Are you assuming that your adviser and committee members know everything about your topic? They might not be the best judges at this point. You are now the expert on your topic.

A: . . . Hmmm. Maybe so. But still they will see that I am still not an expert writer. The language that I use in places is awkward and non-native-like.

B: It is a myth to assume that all native speakers are good writers. Whether you are an L1 or an L2 writer, you can continue polishing the language forever, and it still won't be perfect. Is imperfect language a reason not to turn this dissertation in, do the defense, and get your life back? Plus, after the defense, you will get another chance to adjust things.

A: Well, yes, that's true.

B: But of course at the end of your revision time, when it comes time to submit the final (really final) document, you will go through the same torture, wondering if you got anything wrong, wondering how the phrasing could be polished even further, wondering if the writing seems scholarly enough, fearing that someone important might discover that you are an imposter. I think I shared with you a couple of things on the Imposter Syndrome by Peggy McIntosh (1985, 1989) and Deborah Crusan (2014, 2017). You're in good company. A lot of academics feel like frauds.

A: Aren't all these fears justified?

B: Well, they are normal, but they aren't usually justified. That's why you have to stop. You can go back to the project later, when everything is finished, and after you have rested for about a month, and feel ready maybe to write an article or two from it.

A: I have chances in the future to keep improving everything, is that what you're saying?

B: Of course, assuming that you are not so sick of the project that you don't ever want to look at it again. That happens, you know. You hope you'll continue loving your dissertation and will continue the work in some way, but you might come to hate it. If you decide to move on, so be it.

A: But this is such a high-stakes project! My future depends on it!

B: Your future depends on your submitting a passing dissertation, not a perfect one. Believe me. Once the dissertation is done and turned in, hardly anyone will ever look at it again. They will look at the dissertation-related work that you do after you graduate.

A: That's depressing.

B: That's why you need to get this over with and move on to other things that people really will read, if you want to continue a scholarly life. Articles, books, conference papers. Remember what Judith Meloy (1994) said a long time ago about writing a qualitative doctoral dissertation—the end is the beginning. The same is true for all types of dissertations, I think.

A: So I should start looking ahead now to what I might write next?

B: Yes. This dissertation will give you some status and the "doctor" title, but it's the writings and presentations that come after it that will count.

A: That makes sense. But I am not sure how to make myself stop. I cannot turn in a dissertation draft that has an unfinished feel to it.

B: My point is that it will always feel unfinished. You can make it look and sound more finished than it feels to you by how you revise and polish the final draft. Follow the dissertation template carefully. Make the document pretty. Proofread until you can't focus on the screen or page anymore. Of course you need to hedge your assertions carefully, but you can still take on a tone of finality. Your language will tell readers that the dissertation is coming to an end, but that the inquiry will continue. Your language will also tell readers that although you are now an authority (small "a") on your topic, you don't know everything. You will continue studying. And you might even inspire readers to embark on similar work.

A: Sounds like a tricky bit of writing.

B: It is—how to sound authoritative while saying at the same time that you don't know everything and that your study is incomplete and must continue. And a doctoral dissertation writer is by definition a novice scholar. But you can do it. This is the position that all writers-researchers find themselves in, even at the end of a long career.

A: It sounds like you are saying that I'll never "get there."

B: Right. I think it's impossible. You can continue your inquiry all your life. You'll always be in a position of knowing more today than you did yesterday but not as much as you will tomorrow. Once your learning stops, your intellectual life is over.

A: Got it. This is one sense in which the dissertation represents a beginning, or at least a continuation, rather than an ending, right?

B: Exactly. So finish this up and move on. Get some sleep. Give your carpal tunnel syndrome a break. It's time to plan a graduation party.

References and Resources

Ahern, K., & Manathunga, C. (2004). Clutch-starting stalled research students. *Innovative Higher Education, 28*, 237–254.

Aitchison, C. (2009). Writing groups for doctoral education. *Studies in Higher Education, 34*(8), 905–916.

Aitchison, C., & Guerin, C. (2014). Writing groups, pedagogy, theory and practice: An introduction. In C. Aitchison & C. Guerin (Eds.), *Writing groups for doctoral education and beyond: Innovations in practice and theory* (pp. 3–17). New York: Routledge/Taylor & Francis.

Aitchison, C., & Mowbray, S. (2013). Doctoral women: Managing emotions, managing doctoral studies. *Teaching in Higher Education, 18*(8), 859–870. doi:10.1080/13562517.2013.827642.

Ali, A., & Kohun, F. (2006). Dealing with isolation feelings in IS doctoral programs. *International Journal of Doctoral Studies, 1*, 21–33.

Ali, A., & Kohun, F. (2007). Dealing with social isolation to minimize doctoral attrition: A four stage framework. *International Journal of Doctoral Studies, 2*, 33–49. Retrieved from http://www.ijds.org/Volume2/IJDSv2p033-049Ali28.pdf

APA Manual (see *Publication Manual of the American Psychological Association*)

Badenhorst, C., & Guerin, C. (2016a). Post/graduate research literacies and writing pedagogies. In C. Badenhorst & C. Guerin (Eds.), *Research literacies and writing pedagogies for masters and doctoral writers* (pp. 3–28). Boston: Brill.

Badenhorst, C., & Guerin, C. (2016b). *Research literacies and writing pedagogies for masters and doctoral writers*. Leiden, Netherlands: Brill.

Badenhorst, C. M. (2018). Graduate student writing: Complexity in literature reviews. *Studies in Graduate and Postdoctoral Education, 9*(1), 58–74.

Badenhorst, C., Moloney, C., Rosales, J., Dyer, J., & Ru, L. (2015). Beyond deficit: Graduate student research-writing pedagogies. *Teaching in Higher Education, 20*(1), 1–11.

Baker, V. L., Pifer, M. J., & Griffin, K. A. (2014). Mentor-protégé fit: Identifying and developing effective mentorship across identities in doctoral education. *International Journal for Researcher Development, 5*(2), 83–98.

Barkhuizen, G. (Ed.). (2013). *Narrative research in applied linguistics.* Cambridge, England: Cambridge University Press.

Barkhuizen, G. (2014). Narrative research in language teaching and learning. *Language Teaching, 47*(4), 450–466.

Barnacle, R., & Dall' Alba, G. (2014). Beyond skills: Embodying writerly practices through the doctorate. *Studies in Higher Education, 39*(7), 1139–1149.

Barnacle, R., & Mewburn, I. (2010). Learning networks and the journey of 'becoming doctor.' *Studies in Higher Education, 35*(4), 433–444.

Bazerman, C. (2004). Speech acts, genres, and activity systems: How texts organize activity and people. In C. Bazerman & P. Prior (Eds.), *What writing does and how it does it: An introduction to analyzing texts and textual practices* (pp. 309–339). Mahwah, NJ: Lawrence Erlbaum.

Becker, H. S. (1986). *Writing for social scientists: How to start and finish your thesis, book, or article.* Chicago: University of Chicago Press.

Becker, H. S. (2007). *Writing for social scientists: How to start and finish your thesis, book, or article* (2nd ed.). Chicago: University of Chicago Press.

Becker, H. S. (2020). *Writing for social scientists: How to start and finish your thesis, book, or article* (3rd ed.). Chicago: University of Chicago Press.

Berkenkotter, C., Huckin, T. N., & Ackerman, J. (1991). Social context and socially constructed texts: The initiation of a graduate student into a writing research community. In C. Bazerman & J. Paradis (Eds.), *Textual dynamics of the professions* (pp. 191–215). Madison: University of Wisconsin Press.

Bitchener, J. (2010). *Writing an applied linguistics thesis or dissertation: A guide to presenting empirical research.* London: Palgrave.

Bitchener, J. (2017) *A guide to supervising non-native English writers of theses and dissertations: Focus on the writing process.* New York: Routledge.

Bitchener, J., & Basturkmen, H. (2006). Perceptions of the difficulties of postgraduate L2 thesis students writing the discussion section. *Journal of English for Academic Purposes, 5*(1), 4–18.

Bitchener, J., Basturkmen, H., & East, M. (2010). The focus of supervisor written feedback to thesis/dissertation students. *International Journal of English Studies, 10*(2), 79–97.

Bitchener, J., & Storch, N. (2016). *Written corrective feedback for L2 development.* Bristol, England: Multilingual Matters.

Bitchener, J., Storch, N., & Wette, R. (Eds.). (2017). *Teaching writing for academic purposes to multilingual students: Instructional approaches.* New York: Routledge.

Blakeslee, A. M. (1997), Activity, context, interaction, and authority: Learning to write scientific papers in situ. *Journal of Business and Technical Communication, 11*(2), 125–169.

Blum, L. D. (2010). The "All-But-the-Dissertation" student and the psychology of the doctoral dissertation. *Journal of College Student Psychotherapy, 24*, 74–85.

Boice, R. (1985). Cognitive components of blocking. *Written Communication, 2*(1), 91–44.

Boice, R. (1990). *Professors as writers: A self-help guide to productive writing.* Stillwater, OK: New Forums Press.

Bolker, J. (1998). *Writing your dissertation in fifteen minutes a day: A guide to starting, revising, and finishing your doctoral thesis.* New York: Henry Holt and Co.

Boote, D. N., & Beile, P. (2005). Scholars before researchers: On the centrality of the dissertation literature review in research preparation. *Educational Researcher, 34*(6), 3–15.

Bosanquet, A., & Cahir, J. (2015). "What feelings didn't I experience!" Affect and identity in PhD writing. In C. Badenhorst & C. Guerin (Eds.), *Research literacies and writing pedagogies for masters and doctoral writers* (pp. 132–148). London: Brill.

Botelho de Magalhães, M., Cotterall, S., & Mideros, D. (2019). Identity, voice and agency in two EAL doctoral writing contexts. *Journal of Second Language Writing, 43*, 4–14.

Bruffee, K. A. (1983). Writing and reading as collaborative or social acts. In J. N. Hays, P. A. Roth, J. R. Ramsey, & R. D. Foulke (Eds.), *The writer's mind: Writing as a mode of thinking* (pp. 159–169). Urbana, IL: National Council of Teachers of English.

Bruner, J. (1991). The narrative construction of reality. *Critical Inquiry, 18*, 1–21.

Burford, J. (2017). Conceptualising doctoral writing as affective-political practice. *International Journal of Doctoral Studies, 12*, 18–32. Retrieved from https://www.informingscience.org/Journals/IJDS/Articles

Cadman, K. (1997). Thesis writing for international students: A question of identity? *English for Specific Purposes, 16(*1), 3–14.

Caffarella, R.S., & Barnett, B.G. (2000). Teaching doctoral students to become scholarly writers: The importance of giving and receiving critiques. *Studies in Higher Education, 25*(1), 39–52.

Callary, B., Werthner, P., & Trudel, P. (2012). The lived experience of a doctoral student: The process of learning and becoming. *The Qualitative Report, 1*7(43), 1–20. Retrieved from https://nsuworks.nova.edu/tqr/vol17/iss43/2

Cargill, M. (2000). Intercultural postgraduate supervision meetings: An exploratory discourse study. *Prospect, 15*(2), 28–38.

Cargill, M., & Burgess, S. (Eds.). (2017). *Publishing research in English as an additional language: Practices, pathways and potentials.* Adelaide, Australia: University of Adelaide Press.

Casanave, C. P. (1990). *The role of writing in socializing graduate students into an academic discipline in the social sciences.* Unpublished doctoral dissertation, Stanford University.

Casanave, C. P. (1995). Local interactions: Constructing contexts for composing in a graduate sociology program. In G. Braine & D. Belcher (Eds.), *Academic writing in a second language: Essays on research and pedagogy* (pp. 83–110). Norwood, NJ: Ablex.

Casanave, C. P. (2011). *Journal writing in second language education.* Ann Arbor: University of Michigan Press.

Casanave, C. P. (2014). *Before the dissertation: A textual mentor for doctoral students at early stages of a research project.* Ann Arbor: University of Michigan Press.

Casanave, C. P. (2016). What advisors need to know about the invisible real-life struggles of doctoral dissertation writers. In S. Simpson, N. A. Caplan, M. Cox, & T. Phillips (Eds.), *Supporting graduate student writers: Research, curriculum, and program design* (pp. 97–116). Ann Arbor: University of Michigan Press.

Casanave, C. P. (2019). Performing expertise in doctoral dissertations: Thoughts on a fundamental dilemma facing doctoral students and their supervisors. *Journal of Second Language Writing, 43*, 57–62.

Casanave, C. P., & Li, X. (Eds.). (2008). *Learning the literacy practices of graduate school: Insiders' reflections on academic enculturation*. Ann Arbor: University of Michigan Press.

Casanave, C. P., & Sosa, M. (2008). Getting in line: The challenge (and importance) of speaking and writing about difficult topics. In D. Belcher and A. Hirvela (Eds.), *The oral/literate connection: Perspectives on speaking, writing, and other media interactions* (pp. 87–109). Ann Arbor: University of Michigan Press.

Castro, V., Cavazos, J., Garcia, E. E., & Castro, A. Y. (2011). The road to doctoral success and beyond. *International Journal of Doctoral Studies, 6,* 51–77.

Cheng, A. (2018). *Genre and graduate-level research writing*. Ann Arbor: University of Michigan Press.

Cirillo, F. (2006). *The Pomodoro technique*. http://baomee.info/pdf/technique/1.pdf

Clance, R. R., & Imes, S. (1978). The imposter phenomenon in high achieving women: Dynamics and therapeutic intervention. *Psychotherapy Theory, Research and Practice, 15*(3), 1–9.

Clandinin, D. J., (Ed.). (2007). *Handbook of narrative inquiry: Mapping a methodology*. Thousand Oaks, CA: Sage.

Claremont Graduate University. https://mycampus.cgu.edu/web/writing-rhetoric/home/dissertation-boot-camp

Cohen, A. D., & Carson-Brooks, A. (2001). Research on direct versus translated writing: Students' strategies and their results. *The Modern Language Journal, 85*(2), 169–188.

Cooley, L., & Lewkowicz, J. (Eds.). (2003). *Dissertation writing in practice: Turning ideas into text*. Hong Kong: Hong Kong University Press.

Cornér, S., Löfström, E., & Pyhältö, K. (2017). The relationships between doctoral students' perceptions of supervision and burnout. *International Journal of Doctoral Studies, 12*, 91–106.

Cotterall, S. (2011). Doctoral students writing: Where's the pedagogy? *Teaching in Higher Education, 16*(4), 413–425.

Cotterall, S. (2013). 'More than just a brain: Emotions and the doctoral experience.' *Higher Education Research & Development, 32*(2), 174–187.

Cotterall, S. (2015). The rich get richer: international doctoral candidates and scholarly identity. *Innovations in Education and Teaching International, 52*(4), 360–370.

Council of Graduate Schools (2019). Degree completion. Retrieved from https://cgsnet.org/degree-completion

Creswell, J. W. (2014). *Research design: Qualitative, quantitative, and mixed methods approaches* (4th ed.). Thousand Oaks, CA: Sage.

Creswell, J. W. (2015). *A concise introduction to mixed methods research*. Los Angeles: Sage.

Creswell, J. W. (2016). *30 essential skills for the qualitative researcher*. Los Angeles: Sage.

Crusan, D. (2014, November). Fake it 'till you make it: The imposter syndrome—The dilemma of (women) academics. Plenary at the Symposium on Second Language Writing, Arizona State University, Tempe, AZ.

Crusan, D. J. (2017). Fake it 'til you make it: The imposter syndrome—The dilemma of (women) academics. In P. K. Matsuda, S. E. Snyder, & K. D. O'Meara (Eds.), *Professionalizing second language writing* (pp. 90–110). Anderson, SC: Parlor Press.

Csikszentmihalyi, M. (1990). *Flow: The psychology of optimal experience*. New York: HarperPerennial.

Csikszentmihalyi, M. (1996). *Creativity: Flow and the psychology of discovery and invention*. New York: HarperPerennial.

Davis, J. L. (2000). Graduate school can be bad for your health. *WebMD*. Retrieved from https://www.webmd.com/balance/stress-management/news/20000510/how-stress-affects-graduate-students#1

Dillard, A. (1989). *The writing life*. New York: Harper & Row.

Elbow, P. (1981). *Writing with power*. New York: Oxford University Press.

Elbow, P. (1994). Closing my eyes as I speak: An argument for ignoring audience. In G. Tate, E. P. J. Corbett, & N. Myers (Eds.), *The writing teacher's sourcebook* (3rd ed.), (pp. 258–276). New York: Oxford University Press.

Elbow, P. (1995). Being a writer vs. being an academic: A conflict in goals. *College Composition and Communication, 46*(1), 72–83.

Englander, K. (2009). Transformation of the identities of nonnative English-speaking scientists as a consequence of the social construction of revision. *Journal of Language, Identity & Education, 8*(1), 35–53.

Farkas, D. (n.d.) Cheeky Scientist. Retrieved from https://cheekyscientist.com/insiders-guide-to-write-a-thesis-when-short-on-time/

Farkas, D. (2015, January 19). Why you will not finish your thesis without help. Finish Your Thesis. Retrieved from https://finishyourthesis.com/fail-to-finish-your-thesis/

Farkas, D. (2018, January 4). 7 reasons why bright students drop out of grad school. Finish Your Thesis. Retrieved from https://finishyourthesis.com/drop-out/

Farkas, D. (2019, January 20). 5 steps to stop distractions from derailing your thesis writing. Finish Your Thesis. Retrieved from https://finishyourthesis.com/distractions-thesis-writing/

Feak, C, B., & Swales, J. M. (2009). *Telling a research story: Writing a literature review.* Ann Arbor: University of Michigan Press.

Feather, D., & McDermott, K. E. (2014). The role of new doctoral supervisors in higher education: A reflective view of literature and experience using two case studies. *Research in Post-Compulsory Education, 19*(2), 165–176.

Flower, L., & Hayes, J. (1981). A cognitive process theory of writing. *College Composition and Communication, 32*, 365–387.

Flowerdew, J., & Costley, T. (Eds.). (2017). *Discipline-specific writing: Theory into practice*. New York: Routledge.

French, A., & Kendall, A. (2017). Getting lost (and found) in supervision: An ethnodrama. *Studies in Graduate and Postdoctoral Education, 8*(1), 2–14.

Fujioka, M. (2014). L2 student-U.S. professor interactions through disciplinary writing assignments: An activity theory perspective. *Journal of Second Language Writing, 25*, 40–58.

Fung, A. S. K., Southcott, J., & Siu, F. (2017). Exploring mature-aged students' motives for doctoral study and their challenges: A cross border research collaboration. *International Journal of Doctoral Studies, 12*, 175–195. Retrieved from http://www.informingscience.org/Publications/3790

Galloway, N., & Rose, H. (2015). *Introducing Global Englishes.* New York: Routledge.

Gardiner, M., Tiggemann, M., Kearns, H., & Marshall, K. (2007). Show me the money! An empirical analysis of mentoring outcomes for women in academia. *Higher Education Research & Development, 26*(4), 425–442.

Gardner, H. (1983). *Frames of mind: The theory of multiple intelligences*. New York: Basic Books.

Gardner, S. K. (2008). Fitting the mold of graduate school: A qualitative study of socialization in doctoral education. *Innovative Higher Education, 33*, 125–138.

George, C. E., Saclarides, E. S., Lubienski, S. T. (2018). A difference in priorities?: Why US and international students consider leaving doctoral programs. *Studies in Graduate and Postdoctoral Education, 9*(1), 38–57.

Glatthorn, A. A., & Joyner, R. L. (2005). *Writing the winning thesis or dissertation: A step-by-step guide* (2nd ed.). Thousand Oaks, CA: Corwin Press.

Glatthorn, A. A., Rouse, W. A., & Joyner, R. L. (2013). *Writing the winning thesis or dissertation: A step-by-step guide* (3rd ed.). Thousand Oaks, CA: Corwin Press.

Golde, C. (2000). Should I stay or should I go? Student descriptions of the doctoral attrition process. *Review of Higher Education, 23*, 199–227.

Golde, C. M. (2005). The role of the department and discipline in doctoral student attrition: Lessons from four departments. *Journal of Higher Education, 76*(6), 669–700.

Golde, C. M. Blog: http://gradlogic.org/about/

Goldhill, O. (2015). Multitasking is scientifically impossible, so give up now. Retrieved from https://www.telegraph.co.uk/women/womens-life/11512469/Multitasking-is-scientifically-impossible-so-give-up-now Multitask.html

Gopaul, B. (2016). Applying cultural capital and field to doctoral student socialization. *International Journal for Researcher Development, 7*(1), 46–62.

Gube, J., Getenet, S., Satariyan, A., & Muhammad, Y. (2017). Towards "operating within" the field: Doctoral students' views of supervisors' discipline expertise. *International Journal of Doctoral Studies, 12*, 1–16.

Guerin, C. (2014). The gift of writing groups: Critique, community and confidence. In C. Aitchison & C. Guerin (Eds.), *Writing groups for doctoral education and beyond: Innovations in practice and theory* (pp. 128–142). New York: Routledge/Taylor & Francis.

Guerin, C., Walker, R., Aitchison, C., Laming, M. M., Padmanabhan, M. C., & James, B. (2017). Doctoral supervisor development in Australian universities: Preparing research supervisors to teach writing. *Journal of Academic Language & Learning, 11*(1), A88–A103.

Habibie, P. (2019). To be native or not to be native: That is not the question. In P. Habibie, & K. Hyland, (Eds.), *Novice writers and scholarly publication: Authors, mentors, gatekeepers* (pp. 35–52). Cham, Switzerland: Palgrave MacMillan.

Habibie, P., & Hyland, K. (Eds.). (2019). *Novice writers and scholarly publication: Authors, mentors, gatekeepers*. Cham, Switzerland: Palgrave MacMillan.

Halse, C., & Malfroy, J. (2010). Retheorizing doctoral supervision as professional work. *Studies in Higher Education, 35*(1), 79–92.

Halse, C. (2011). 'Becoming a supervisor': The impact of doctoral supervision on the learning of supervisors. *Studies in Higher Education, 36*(5), 557–570.

Hartse, J. H., & Kubota, R. (2014). Pluralizing English? Variation in high-stakes academic texts and challenges of copyediting. *Journal of Second Language Writing, 24*, 71–82.

Harvard Health Publishing, n.d. https://www.health.harvard.edu.

Harwood, N., & Petrič, B. (2016). *Experiencing Master's supervision: Perspectives of international students and their supervisors*. London: Taylor & Francis.

Holliday, A. (2009). English as a lingua franca: 'Non-native speakers' and cosmopolitan realities. In F. Sharifian, (Ed.), *English as an international language: Perspectives and pedagogical issues* (pp. 21–33). Bristol, England: Multilingual Matters.

Hopwood, N. (2010). A sociocultural view of doctoral students' relationships and agency. *Studies in Continuing Education, 32*(2), 103–117.

Huerta, M., Goodson, P., Beigi, M., & Chlup, D. (2017). Graduate students as academic writers: Writing anxiety, self-efficacy and emotional intelligence. *Higher Education Research & Development, 36*(4), 716–729.

Hutchinson, S., Lawrence, H., & Filipovic-Carter, D. (2014). *Enhancing the doctoral experience: A guide for supervisors and their international students*. Burlington, VT: Gower Publishing Company.

Hyland, K. (2015). *Academic publishing: Issues and challenges in the construction of knowledge*. Oxford, England: Oxford University Press.

Ingleton, C., & Cadman, K. (2002). Silent issues for international postgraduate research students: Emotion and agency in academic success. *Australian Educational Researcher, 29*, 93–113.

Ivanič, R. (1998). *Writing and identity: The discoursal construction of identity in academic writing.* Philadelphia: John Benjamins.

Jairam, D., & Kahl, D. H. Jr. (2012). Navigating the doctoral experience: The role of social support in successful degree completion. *International Journal of Doctoral Studies 7,* 311–329.

Jazvac-Martek, M., Chen, S., & McAlpine, L. (2011). Tracking the doctoral experience over time: Cultivating agency in diverse spaces. In L. McAlpine & C. Amundsen (Eds.). *Doctoral education: Research-based strategies for doctoral students, supervisors and administrators* (pp. 17–36). New York: Springer.

Jenkins, J. (2014). *English as a lingua franca in the international university: The politics of academic English language policy.* Abingdon, England: Routledge.

Joyner, R., L., Rouse, W. A., & Glatthorn, A. A. (2018). *Writing the winning thesis or dissertation: A step-by-step guide* (4th ed.). Thousand Oaks, CA: Corwin.

Junco, R., & Cotten, S. R. (2012). No A4 U: The relationship between multitasking and academic performance. *Computers & Education, 59*(2), 505–514.

Kachru, B. B. (Ed.). (1992). *The other tongue: English across cultures* (2nd ed.). Urbana: University of Illinois Press.

Kachru, B. B. (1997). World Englishes and English-using communities. *Annual Review of Applied Linguistics, 17*, 66–87.

Kachru, B. B., Kachru, Y., & Nelson, C. L. (Eds.). (2006). *The handbook of World Englishes.* Malden, MA: Blackwell.

Kamler, B., & Thomson, P. (2007). Rethinking doctoral writing as text work and identity work. In B. Somekh & T. Schwandt (Eds.), *Knowledge production: Research work in interesting times* (pp. 166–179). New York: Routledge.

Kamler, B., & Thomson, P. (2008). The failure of dissertation advice books: Toward alternative pedagogies for doctoral writing. *Educational Researcher, 37*(8), 507–514.

Kamler, B., & Thomson, P. (2014). *Helping doctoral students write: Pedagogies for supervision* (2nd ed.). Oxon, England: Routledge.

Kearns, H., Forbes, A., Gardiner, M., & Marshall, K. (2008). When a high distinction isn't good enough: A review of perfectionism and self-handicapping. *The Australian Educational Researcher, 35*(3), 21–36.

Kearns, H., Gardiner, M., & Marshall, K. (2008). Innovation in PhD completion: The hardy shall succeed (and be happy!). *Higher Education Research & Development, 27*(1), 77–89.

Kilbourn, B. (2006). The qualitative doctoral dissertation proposal. *Teachers College Record, 108*(4), 529–576.

Kiley, M. (2017). Reflections on change in doctoral education: An Australian case study. *Studies in Graduate and Postdoctoral Education, 8*(2), 78–87.

Kobayashi, H., & Rinnert, C. (1992). Effects of first language on second language writing: Translation versus direct composition. *Language Learning, 42*(2), 183–209.

Krathwohl, D. R., & Smith, N. L. (2005). *How to prepare a dissertation proposal: Suggestions for students in education and the social and behavioral sciences.* Syracuse: Syracuse University Press.

Kumar, S., & Johnson, M. (2017). Mentoring doctoral students online: Mentor strategies and challenges. *Mentoring & Tutoring: Partnership in Learning, 25*(2), 202–222.

Kumar, V., & Stracke, E. (2007). An analysis of written feedback on a PhD thesis. *Teaching in Higher Education, 12*(4), 461–470.

Kumar, V., & Stracke, E. (2011). Examiners' reports on theses: Feedback or assessment? *Journal of English for Academic Purposes, 10*(4), 211–222.

Kurtz-Costes, B., Andrews Helmke, L., & Ülkü-Steiner, B. (2006). Gender and doctoral studies: The perceptions of PhD students in an American university. *Gender and Education, 18*(2), 137–155.

Kwan, B. S. C. (2008). The nexus of reading, writing and researching in the doctoral undertaking of humanities and social sciences: Implications for literature reviewing. *English for Specific Purposes, 27*(1), 42–56.

Kwan, B. S. C. (2009). Reading in preparation for writing a PhD thesis: Case studies of experiences. *Journal of English for Academic Purposes, 8*(3), 180–191.

Lanham, R. (2007). *Style: An anti-textbook.* Philadelphia: Paul Dry Books.

Lave, J., & Wenger, E. (1991). *Situated learning: Legitimate peripheral participation*. Cambridge, England: Cambridge University Press.

Lee, A. (2008). How are doctoral students supervised? Concepts of doctoral research supervision. *Studies in Higher Education, 33*(3), 267–281.

Lee, J. J. (2018, January 8). The not-so-secret guide to dissertating. *Chronicle of Higher Education*. Retrieved from https://www.chronicle.com/article/The-Not-So-Secret-Guide-to/242186?fbclid=IwAR2NiTam22lsUHo53k4U-4Ctz1P1LjTM5hqW10IixYnKZ-OdB7-VdDDvEao

Lei, J. & Hu, G. (2015). Apprenticeship in scholarly publishing: A student perspective on doctoral supervisors' roles. *Publications, 3*(1), 27–42.

Levecque, K., Anseel, F., De Beuckelaer, A., Van der Heyden, J., & Gisle, L. (2017). Work organization and mental health problems in PhD students. *Research Policy, 46*, 868–879.

Li, S., & Seale, C. (2007). Managing criticism in Ph.D. supervision: A qualitative case study. *Studies in Higher Education, 32*(4), 511–526.

Li, Y. (2015). "Publish SCI papers or no degree": Practices of Chinese doctoral supervisors in response to the publication pressure on science students. *Asia Pacific Journal of Education, 36*, 545–558.

Li, Y. (2019). Mentoring junior scientists for research publication. In P. Habibie & K. Hyland (Eds.), *Novice writers and scholarly publication: Authors, mentors, gatekeepers* (pp. 233–250). Cham, Switzerland: Palgrave MacMillan.

Lillis, T., & Curry, M. J. (2018). Trajectories of knowledge and desire: Multilingual women scholars researching and writing in academia. *Journal of English for Academic Purposes, 32*, 53–66.

Lindsay, S. (2015). What works for doctoral students in completing their thesis? *Teaching in Higher Education, 20*(2), 183–196.

Locke, L. F., Spirduso, W. W., & Silverman, S. J. (2017). *Proposals that work: A guide for planning dissertations and grant proposals* (5th ed.). Thousand Oaks, CA: Sage.

Lovitts, B.E. (2001). *Leaving the ivory tower: The causes and consequences of departure from doctoral study*. Lanham, MD: Rowman & Littlefield.

Lovitts, B. E., & Nelson, C. (2000). The hidden crisis in graduate education: Attrition from Ph.D. programs. *Academe, 86*(6), 44.

Lu, S. (2015). Blast through writer's block. Retrieved from https://www.apa.org/gradpsych/2015/11/writers-block

Ma, L. P. F. (2019). Academic writing support through individual consultations: EAL doctoral student experiences and evaluation. *Journal of Second Language Writing, 43*, 72–79.

Maher, M., Feldon, D., Timmerman, B., & Chao, J. (2014). Faculty perceptions of common challenges encountered by novice doctoral writers. *Higher Education Research and Development, 33*(4), 699–711.

Maher, M. A., Ford, M. E., & Thompson, C. M. (2004). Degree progress of women doctoral students: Factors that constrain, facilitate, and differentiate. *The Review of Higher Education, 27*(3), 385–408.

Manathunga, C. (2005). Early warning signs in postgraduate research education: A different approach to ensuring timely completions. *Teaching in Higher Education, 10*(2), 219–233. doi:10.1080/1356251042000337963

Manathunga, C. (2014). Reflections on working with doctoral students across and between cultures and languages. In S. Carter & L. Deborah (Eds.), *Developing generic support for doctoral students: Practice and pedagogy* (pp. 71–74). New York: Routledge.

Marias, D. (2016, September 13). Strategies to maintain focus while writing your dissertation. *Gradhacker blog*. Retrieved from http://www.insidehighered.com/blogs/gradhacker/strategies-maintain-focus-while-writing-your-dissertation

Maxwell, J. A. (2006). Literature reviews of, and for, educational research: A commentary on Boote and Beile's "Scholars Before Researchers." *Educational Researcher, 35*(9), 28–31.

McAlpine, L. (2017). Building on success? Future challenges for doctoral education globally. *Studies in Graduate and Postdoctoral Education, 8*(2), 66–77.

McAlpine, L., & Amundsen, C. (Eds.). (2011). *Doctoral education: Research-based strategies for doctoral students, supervisors and administrators*. Dordrecht, The Netherlands: Springer.

McIntosh, P. (1985). *Work in progress: Feeling like a fraud*. Wellesley, MA: The Stone Center.

McIntosh, P. (1989). *Feeling like a fraud: Part II*. Work in Progress #37. MA: The Stone Center.

McKinley, J., & Rose, H. (2018). Conceptualizations of language errors, standards, norms, and nativeness in English for research publication purposes: An analysis of journal submission guidelines. *Journal of Second Language Writing, 42*, 1–11.

McMullan, J. (2018). Becoming a researcher: Re-inventing writing spaces. *Journal of English for Academic Purposes, 32*, 21–32.

Meloy, J. M. (1994). *Writing the qualitative dissertation: Understanding by doing.* Mahwah, NJ: Lawrence Erlbaum.

Meloy, J. M. (2002). *Writing the qualitative dissertation: Understanding by doing (2nd ed.).* Mahwah, NJ: Lawrence Erlbaum.

Merton, R. K. (1967). *On theoretical sociology: Five essays old and new.* New York: Free Press.

Mewburn, I. (2010, October 26). The loneliness of the long distance thesis writer. *Thesis Whisperer* blog. Retrieved from https://thesiswhisperer.com/2010/10/26/the-loneliness-of-the-long-distance-thesis-writer/

Mewburn, I. (2019a). *How to tame your PhD* (2nd ed.). Acton, Australia: Thesis Whisperer Books. https://www.amazon.com/Tame-Your-Thesis-Whisperer-Books-ebook/dp/B009GPRSP0

Mewburn, I. (2019b). *Becoming an academic: How to get through grad school and beyond.* Baltimore: Johns Hopkins University Press.

Mochizuki, N. (2019). The lived experience of thesis writers in group writing conferences: The quest for "perfect" and "critical." *Journal of Second Language Writing, 43*, 36–35.

Morton, J., & Storch, N. (2019). Developing an authorial voice in PhD multilingual student writing: The reader's perspective. *Journal of Second Language Writing, 43*, 15–23.

Mulholland, J. (2011). What I've learned about revising a dissertation. *Journal of Scholarly Publishing, 43*(1), 39–51.

Murray, N., & Beglar, D. (2009). *Inside track: Writing dissertations and theses.* Harlow, England: Pearson Education.

Nadler, R. (2011). Blog. Where did my IQ points go? https://www.psychologytoday.com/us/blog/leading-emotional-intelligence/201104/where-did-my-iq-points-go

Nystrand, M. (1989). A social-interactive model of writing. *Written Communication, 6*(1), 66–85.

Onwuegbuzie, A. J., & Collins, K. M. T. (2001). Writing apprehension and academic procrastination among graduate students. *Perceptual and Motor Skills, 92*, 560–562.

Paltridge, B. (2002). Thesis and dissertation writing: An examination of published advice and actual practice. *English for Specific Purposes, 21*, 125–143.

Paltridge, B. (2016). Writing retreats as writing pedagogy. *Writing & Pedagogy, 8*(1), 199–213.

Paltridge, B., & Starfield, S. (2007). *Thesis and dissertation writing in a second language: A handbook for supervisors*. New York: Routledge.

Paltridge, B., & Starfield, S. (2019). *Thesis and dissertation writing in a second language. A handbook for students and their supervisors (2nd ed.)*. London: Routledge.

Paltridge, B., Starfield, S., & Tardy, C. M. (2016). *Ethnographic perspectives on academic writing*. Oxford, England: Oxford University Press.

Paltridge, B., & Woodrow, L. (2012). Thesis and dissertation writing: Moving beyond the text. In R. Tang (Ed.), *Academic writing in a second or foreign language: Issues and challenges facing ESL/EFL academic writers in higher education contexts* (pp. 88–104). London: Continuum.

Paré, A. (2011). Speaking of writing: Supervisory feedback and the dissertation. In L. McAlpine and C. Amundsen (Eds.), *Doctoral education: Research-based strategies for doctoral students, supervisors and administrators* (pp. 59–74). Dordrecht, The Netherlands: Springer.

Paré, A. (2017). Re-thinking the dissertation and doctoral supervision / Reflexiones sobre la tesis doctoral y su supervisión, *Infancia y Aprendizaje, 40*(3), 407–428.

Paré, A. (2019). Re-writing the doctorate: New contexts, identities, and genres. *Journal of Second Language Writing, 43*, 80–84.

Paré, A., Starke-Meyerring, D., & McAlpine, L. (2009). The dissertation as multigenre: Many readers, many readings. In C. Bazerman, A. Bonini, & D. Figueiredo (Eds.), *Genre in a changing world* (pp. 179–193). West Lafayette, IN: Parlor Press.

Perlmutter, D. D. (2015). The completion agenda, Part 3: Revising your dissertation. *Chronicle of Higher Education*. Retrieved from https://www.chronicle.com/article/The-Completion-Agenda-Part-3-/231339

Pinker, S. (2014). *The sense of style: The thinking person's guide to writing in the 21st century*. New York: Viking.

Preece, S. (2018). Identity work in the academic writing classroom: Where gender meets social class. *Journal of English for Academic Purposes, 32*, 9–20.

Prior, P. (1995). Tracing authoritative and internally persuasive discourses: A case study of response, revision, and disciplinary enculturation. *Research in the Teaching of English, 29*(3), 288–325.

Prior, P. A. (1998). *Writing/disciplinarity: A sociohistoric account of literate activity in the academy.* Mahwah, NJ: Lawrence Erlbaum.

Prior, P. (2006). A sociocultural theory of writing. In C. A. MacArthur, S. Graham, & J. Fitzgerald (Eds.), *Handbook of writing research* (pp. 54–66). New York: The Guilford Press.

Publication manual of the American Psychological Association (6th ed.). (2010). Washington, DC: American Psychological Association.

Publication manual of the American Psychological Association (7th ed.). (2020). Washington, DC: American Psychological Association.

Quinlan, K. M. (2013). Writing the first person singular. *Qualitative Inquiry, 19*(5), 405.

Riessman, C. K. (2008). *Narrative methods for the human sciences.* Thousand Oaks, CA: Sage.

Rockinson-Szapkiw, A. J., & Spaulding, L. S. (Eds.). (2014). *Navigating the doctoral journey: A handbook of strategies for success.* Lanham, MD: Rowman & Littlefield.

Rockinson-Szapkiw, A. J., Spaulding, L. S., & Lunde, R. (2017). Women in distance doctoral programs: How they negotiate their identities as mothers, professionals, and academics in order to persist. *International Journal of Doctoral Studies, 12*, 49–72.

Rockinson-Szapkiw, A. J., Spaulding, L. S., Swezey, J. A., & Wicks, C. (2014). Poverty and persistence: A model for understanding individuals' pursuit and persistence in a doctor of education program. *International Journal of Doctoral Studies, 9*, 181–190. Retrieved from http://ijds.org/Volume9/IJDSv9p181-203Rockinson0606.pdf

Rockquemore, K. A. (2016, August 3). How to finish your dissertation. *Inside Higher Education.* Retrieved from https://www.insidehighered.com/advice/2016/08/03/advice-graduate-students-having-difficulty-finishing-their-dissertations-essay

Rose, M. (1980). Rigid rules, inflexible plans, and the stifling of language: A cognitivist analysis of writer's block. *College Composition and Communication*, 31(4), 389–401.

Rose, M. (1984). *Writer's block: The cognitive dimension.* Carbondale: Southern Illinois University Press.

Rose, M. (Ed.). (1985). *When a writer can't write: Studies in writer's block and other composing problems.* New York: The Guilford Press.

Roulston, K., Teitelbaum, D., Chang, B., & Butchart, R. (2016). Strategies for developing a writing community for doctoral students. *International Journal for Researcher Development,* 7(2), 198–210.

Russell-Pinson, L., & Harris, M. L. (2019). Anguish and anxiety, stress and strain: Attending to writers' stress in the dissertation process. *Journal of Second Language Writing, 43*, 63–71.

Russell-Pinson, L., & Jafarian, H. (2020). From avoidance to action: Helping dissertation writers manage procrastination. In S. Madden, M. Eodice, K. T. Edwards Williams, & A. Lockett (Eds.), *Learning from the lived experiences of graduate student writers* (pp. 174–197). Logan: Utah State University Press.

Sakurai, Y., Pyhältö, K., & Lindblom-Ylänne, S. (2012). Factors affecting international doctoral students' academic engagement, satisfaction with their studies, and dropping out. *International Journal for Researcher Development, 3*(2), 99–117.

Salvucci, D. D., & Taatgen, N. A. (2008). Threaded cognition: An integrated theory of concurrent multitasking. *Psychological Review, 115*, 101–130.

Salvucci, D. D., & Taatgen, N. A. (2011). *The multitasking mind.* New York: Oxford University Press.

Sánchez-Martín, C., & Seloni, L. (2019). Transdisciplinary becoming as a gendered activity: A reflexive study of dissertation mentoring. *Journal of Second Language Writing, 43*, 24–35.

Seidlhofer, B. (2011). *Understanding English as a lingua franca.* New York: Oxford University Press.

Silvia, P. J. (2018). *How to write a lot: A practical guide to productive academic writing* (2nd ed.). Washington, DC: American Psychological Association.

Simpson, S., Caplan, N. A., Cox, K., & Phillips, T. (Eds.). (2016). *Supporting graduate student writers: Research, curriculum and program design.* Ann Arbor: University of Michigan Press.

Skakni, I., & McAlpine, L. (2017). Post-PhD researchers' experiences: An emotionally rocky road. *Studies in Graduate and Postdoctoral Education, 8*(2), 205–219.

Sommers, N. (2006). Across the drafts. *College Composition and Communication, 58*(2), 248–257.

Sosin, L. S., & Thomas, J. C. (2014). Managing stress and burnout. In A. J. Rockinson-Szapkiw, & L. S. Spaulding (Eds.). *Navigating the doctoral journey: A handbook of strategies for success* (pp. 55–64). London: Rowman & Littlefield.

Spaulding, L. S., & Rockinson-Szapkiw, A. J. (2012). Hearing their voices: Factors doctoral candidates attribute to their persistence. *International Journal of Doctoral Studies 7,* 199–219.

Starfield, S., & Ravelli, L. J. (2006). "The writing of this thesis was a process that I could not explore with the positivistic detachment of the classical sociologist": Self and structure in New Humanities research theses. *Journal of English for Academic Purposes, 5*(3), 222– 243.

Sternberg, D. (1981). *How to complete and survive a doctoral dissertation.* New York: St. Martin's Press.

Sternberg, R. J. (1988). *The triarchic mind: A new theory of human intelligence.* New York: Penguin Books.

Sternberg, R. J. (1999). Intelligence as developing expertise. *Contemporary Educational Psychology, 24*, 359–375.

Starke-Meyerring, D., Paré, A., Sun, K., & El-Bezre, N. (2014). Probing normalized institutional discourses about writing: The case of the doctoral thesis. *Journal of Academic Language & Learning, 8*(2), 13–27.

Stracke, E., & Kumar, V. (2010). Feedback and self-regulated learning: Insights from supervisors' and PhD examiners' reports. *Reflective Practice, 11*(1), 19–32.

Straforini, C. M. (2015). Dissertation as life chapter: Managing emotions, relationships, and time. *Journal of College Student Psychotherapy, 29*(4), 296–313.

Strandler, O., Johansson, T., Wisker, G., & Claesson, S. (2014). Supervisor or counsellor? – Emotional boundary work in supervision. *International Journal for Researcher Development, 5*(2), 70–82.

Sverdlik, A., Hall, N. C., McAlpine, L., & Hubbard, K. (2018). The PhD experience: A review of the factors influencing doctoral students' completion, achievement, and well-being. *International Journal of Doctoral Studies, 13,* 361–388.

Swales, J. M. (2004). *Research genres: Explorations and applications.* Cambridge, England: Cambridge University Press.

Swales, J. M., & Feak, C. B. (2012). *Academic writing for graduate students: Essential tasks and skills* (3rd ed.). Ann Arbor: University of Michigan Press.

Swales, J. M., & Lindemann, S. (2002). Teaching the literature review to international graduate students. In A. M. Johns, (Ed.). *Genre in the classroom: Multiple perspectives* (pp. 105–119). Mahwah, NJ: Lawrence Erlbaum.

Sword, H. (2009). Writing higher education differently: A manifesto on style. *Studies in Higher Education, 34*(3), 319–336.

Sword, H. (2012). *Stylish academic writing.* Cambridge, MA: Harvard University Press.

Sword, H. (2017). *Air & light & time & space: How successful academics write.* Cambridge, MA: Harvard University Press.

Tavakoli, M., Ghadiri, M., & Zabihi, R. (2014). Direct versus translated writing: The effect of translation on learners' second language writing ability. *GEMA Online Journal of Language Studies, 14*(2).

Thompson, P. (2012). Achieving a voice of authority in PhD theses. In K. Hyland, & C. Sancho Guinda (Eds.), *Stance and voice in written academic genres* (pp. 117–133). New York: Palgrave Macmillan.

Toor, R. (2011, September 6). The problem is: You write too well. *Chronicle of Higher Education.* Retrieved from http://chronicle.com/article/The-Problem-Is-You-Write-Too/128860/

Turley, N. (2013). Mental health issues among graduate students. *Inside Higher Ed.* Retrieved from https://www.insidehighered.com/blogs/gradhacker/mental-health-issues-among-graduate-students

Van Rooij, E., Fokkens-Bruinsma, M., & Jansen, E. (2019). Factors that influence PhD candidates' success: The importance of PhD project characteristics. *Studies in Continuing Education.* doi: 10.1080/0158037X.2019.1652158

Vekkaila, J., Pyhältö, K., & Lonka, K. (2014). Engaging and disengaging doctoral experiences in the behavioural sciences. *International Journal for Researcher Development, 5*(1), 33–55.

Vilkinas, T. (2008). An exploratory study of the supervision of Ph.D./Research students' theses. *Innovative Higher Education, 32*, 297–311.

Wang, T., & Li, L. Y. (2011). 'Tell me what to do' vs. 'guide me through it': Feedback experiences of international doctoral students. *Active Learning in Higher Education, 12*(2), 101–112.

Watson, G. C., & Betts, A. S. (2010). Confronting otherness: An e-conversation between doctoral students living with the Imposter Syndrome. *Canadian Journal for New Scholars in Education/Revue canadienne des jeunes chercheures et chercheurs en education, 3*(1), 1–13.

Webster, M. (2008, May 6). Can you catch up on lost sleep? *Scientific American.* Retrieved from https://www.scientificamerican.com/article/fact-or-fiction-can-you-catch-up-on-sleep/

Wellington, J. (2010). More than a matter of cognition: An exploration of affective writing problems of post-graduate students and their possible solutions. *Teaching in Higher Education, 15*(2), 135–150.

Wellington, J. J., Bathmaker, A.-M., Hunt, C., McCulloch, G., & Sikes, P. (Eds.). (2005). *Succeeding with your doctorate.* Thousand Oaks, CA: Sage.

White, B. (2011). *Mapping your thesis: The comprehensive manual of theory and techniques for masters and doctoral research.* Victoria, Australia: ACER Press/Australian Council for Educational Research Ltd.

Williams, J. M. (1997). *Style: Ten lessons in clarity and grace* (5th ed.). New York: Longman.

Williams, J. M., & Bizup, J. (2015). *Style: The basics of clarity and grace* (11th? ed.). New York: Pearson Education.

Williams, J. M., & Colomb, G. G. (2012). *Style: The basics of clarity and grace.* London: Longman.

Wisker, G., & Robinson, G. (2016). Supervisor wellbeing and identity: challenges and strategies. *International Journal for Researcher Development,* 7(2), 123–140.

Wolcott, H. (1990). *Writing up qualitative research.* Newbury Park, CA: Sage.

Wolcott, H. F. (2001). *The art of fieldwork.* Walnut Creek, CA: Altamira Press.

Wright, T., & Cochrane, R. (2000). Factors influencing successful submission of PhD theses. *Studies in Higher Education, 25*(2), 181–195.

Zamel, V. (1982). Writing: The process of discovering meaning. *TESOL Quarterly, 16*(2), 195–209.

Zamel, V. (1983). The composing process of advanced ESL students: Six case studies. *TESOL Quarterly, 17*(2), 165–187.

Zhao, C.-M., Golde, C. M., & McCormick, A. C. (2007). More than a signature: How advisor choice and advisor behaviour affect doctoral student satisfaction. *Journal of Further and Higher Education, 31*(3), 263–281.

Zinsser, W. (2006). *On writing well: The classic guide to writing nonfiction* (30th Anniversary Ed.). New York: Harper Collins.

Zinsser, W. (2012). *On writing well: The classic guide to writing nonfiction* (30th Anniversary Ed.). New York: Collins Reference.

Subject Index

Author Index